Dear Young U,
Don't lose you
event that you've lost your way
Please remember...

God loves you,

You are beautifully created,

you are the only one that can be you,

And you matter ♡

I love you ♡

Dear Young Woman

There's Triumph After the Trial

ALANDRIA LLOYD

Copyright 2019 Alandria Lloyd

All rights reserved. No part of this book may be reproduced in any form or by any electronic or mechanical means, including information storage and retrieval systems, without written permission by the author, Alandria Lloyd.

CONTENTS

Introduction 1

1. Tar Baby 5
2. I Still Remember 11
3. Storms That Build 17
4. The Sunken Place 25
5. Too Desperate for Love 31
6. Blindsided 37
7. Broken into Beautiful 43
8. Lost and Found 49
9. Protective Custody 55
10. You Are Valuable 61
11. Against the Grain 67
12. You Are Worthy of God's Best 73
13. Bruised, Shattered, Broken, but Blessed 79
14. Releasing What Once Held Me Emotionally Captive ... 85
15. Don't Lose Your Way 91
16. Love Yourself and Know Your Worth 97

17. The Secret She Kept 103

18. The Love That Taught Me Self Love 109

19. Indestructible Woman of Grace... 115

20. Cycles Are Meant to Be Broken 121

21. Thank God for Growth 127

22. Empty Place.. 133

23. Never Looking Back 139

24. Do I Still Have Value After HIV 145

25. Rejection Veil 151

26. Nothing Happened... 157

Introduction

There are rumors that suggest that women can't work together or that women are fake. In some cases, this may be true, however I strongly believe that many women have issues working together due to fear. Fear that says, "Don't let anyone get too close because they may stab you in the back."

Some women don't allow others to get close for fear of what they may see, as opposed to what they may do. You see, when you hide unresolved parts of your past or work hard to hold up the mask that covers the pain in your eyes, you can become fearful that others may see the "real you".

That fear is only real when you haven't accepted who you are or what you have allowed to transpire in your life. Many women are embarrassed about the times they played the fool for love; and some are ashamed to accept and admit that they tolerated more than they

should have in relationships. Then there's another group who feel like they have failed in life and can't see how things will get better.

These are the areas we as women work hard to hide, but the key is acceptance. Yes, it happened, but you are still alive, which means you have a chance to try to do things a better way. The women of "Dear Young Woman" came together to uncover parts of themselves. The secrets that were once concealed are now being revealed.

It's our hope that we as women can bridge the gap by coming together and truly building a sisterhood; one that is unbreakable because of trust and because we refuse to allow anyone to hold our past against us.

It's time to embrace our flaws and encourage one another during the trials of life. We can all work together by sharing pieces of our testimonies to show others that they aren't alone, and that we can relate to their struggles.

Titus 2:3 reminds us that older women should teach the younger women. My question is, how can we teach other women if we won't be transparent and talk to one another regarding the issues of life?

The authors of Dear Young Woman are doing just that, transparently breaking the silence by evoking honest dialogue among women. Sis, I hope you are ready! The stories in this book may make you cry. You may read a testimony and wonder how we knew that you too have experienced the same situation. More than anything, the pages in this book will encourage and comfort you to know that you aren't alone; and that there are women across the world who feel your pain and want to inspire you along your journey. So get comfortable, throw on a t-shirt and an old pair of sweats, get a cup of coffee, and prepare to be inspired.

Tar Baby

As I stared up from the floor of my closet at my clothing rack, I questioned whether it would hold my weight. If I could tie my red, snakeskin belt to it after wrapping it around my neck and be free, let go. Leave it all behind. After all, it seemed way easier than facing the hate that had utterly consumed me. Growing up, I hated mirrors. I'd quickly walk past them in stores, restrooms, and at home.

You see, I was a TAR BABY. Darkie. Blacky. Oil Stain. Midnight. My skin was dark, forehead big, eyes large, and puberty was not exactly a "glow up" for me.

My coping mechanism became talking about myself. Cracking jokes OR "ribbing" myself before others could. For years I tore myself apart; avoiding the pain that began to grow exponentially. Not knowing the whole time, I was erasing my identity.

One experience, in particular, sank my confidence in my early teen years. My cousin had a friend that I thought was so cute. He'd speak when he passed down my street, stop and talk to me, and we even spoke on the phone a few times (back then that was MAJOR). So, mustering up the courage and confidence, I asked my cousin to put in a good word for me or "Hook me up". A couple of days passed, and I hadn't heard anything. My cousin finally returned with an abrupt, "Oh, he said you were pretty for a dark-skinned girl, but he doesn't mess with dark-skinned girls." I was crushed.

Eventually, I began to settle for whatever attention I could from the opposite sex. I engaged in abusive "relationships" at a young age. I didn't believe that I was worthy of much else. I settled because I was "pretty for a dark-skinned girl." I gave so much of myself away because I didn't know I was worth anything.

Before I entered into adulthood, there were many instances of sexual, physical, and verbal abuse that occurred in my young life. Matter of fact, allowing abuse became the norm in my life. I permitted it because at least I was getting attention. I was utterly oblivious to the decay that festered inside of me.

I proudly graduated high school and went off to college, still feeling the same. In fact, that was the time when my self-hate began to get worse. I remember approaching a group's recruitment table in anticipation only to be told, "Oh, we aren't for dark-skinned girls." My mind was blown to pieces. I was rendered speechless. The same scene from my neighborhood days seemed to be happening to me all over again.

Well into my adult life, I continued the battle with confidence and identity issues. I would automatically assume I didn't fit into certain circles because of how I looked in comparison to the appearance of others. I would count myself out of certain opportunities. I didn't believe that I deserved praise nor accolades for my accomplishments. Some social media sites were pure HELL. It was scroll, like, compare, sulk, repeat.

I had a husband, beautiful children, and was walking in my purpose, but it still wasn't enough. The hate was rotting me from the inside out. You see, self-hate is entirely different from prejudices and racism. When someone doesn't like you because of your race, gender, or personal preferences, you can avoid them. However, there is no logoff, deactivate, or block button to prevent self-hate. You have to look in that mirror and see yourself. Look in the eyes of your worst enemy. I never knew I needed to heal until healing was the only option I had if I wanted to live *freely*.

I began the fight for my life. I sat on that floor. My legs asleep, palms sweaty, mind racing, and tears streaming down my cheeks. I sat with myself for hours. I couldn't utter the words to pray. I just cried. No, I sobbed. It was at that moment; I killed myself. Not in the sense you're thinking. I died to who I once was. I murdered that little girl that was desperate to be seen, so she allowed herself to be used and abused. I slaughtered the opinions of those who said I wasn't qualified, called, or good enough.

The place where I contemplated ending it all became my new beginning. As I look back, I realize that I did end it all that day. I ended self-doubt, self-hate, and I had to unlearn and relearn my worth. I learned that I had to give myself what I wanted before I could expect it from someone else. I had to love myself first. I had to value myself first. I had to put myself first. I had to piece myself back together.

Dear Young Woman,

YOU ARE BEAUTIFUL. You are ENOUGH. You are worthy. Do not let the standards and opinions of others shape how you see yourself. Make your bad better, your better best, and your best outstanding. Love yourself before you give your love away to ANYONE else. I urge you to get a pen and paper and write an open letter to those you need to forgive, including *yourself*. Think of those whose offenses and wrongdoings have power over you. How do you know it has power over you? If you think of it and it makes you cry, cuss, or lust--it has power, sis.

LET IT ALL OUT on that paper. Hold nothing back. Forgive them for what was done to you, specifically. Be honest, pure, and forgive yourself. Then, make a pact between yourself, that paper, and GOD that you will never let anyone or anything take you back to those dark spaces and places in time. Walk with your head and your standards *high*. Most importantly, never pass a mirror without flashing yourself a smile.

#

Tyroneca Griffin is a Louisiana native who always had a passion for writing. From a young age, she was an avid reader and wrote endlessly. Her desire to help others evolved into a career in education.

She uses real- life experiences to lead and inspire her students. For the past six years, she has taught middle school and extends her teaching beyond the classroom through coaching.

Tyroneca believes every moment is a teachable moment and considers herself to be a lifelong learner. She walks in her purpose daily and aspires to be what she needed growing up as a young woman.

Contact Info:

Email: tyroneca.booker@selu.edu

Facebook: https://www.facebook.com/tyroneca.bookergriffin

2

I Still Remember...

I still remember the day my husband and I found out we were pregnant. It came at a time in our lives when we felt so much hope in God and in our marriage. We had recently overcome some hardships in our marriage, including struggling with trust issues and insecurities related to some women from my husband's past. Now we were more in love than we had ever been, and the sparks were flying! Since God had begun restoring us and our marriage, we felt it was time to start trying for another baby, more specifically a son.

My husband had a son before we met, but he died tragically when he was only four years old in a house fire. This left my husband scarred for many years. So for me, going into my marriage, I knew how special it would be for me to be the one to birth this child with my husband. What better gift to my husband than to give him something he was missing and desired so strongly? Our youngest daughter had turned one and my husband, who is eight years my senior, said to me, "It's either now or never." So, we decided to just go for it. As apprehensive as I was about having two young kids so close together all while juggling work full-time, ministry, business and managing the lives of our other four kids, we decided to trust God and go for it.

On November 6, 2018 we received our ultrasound confirmation that we were five weeks and four days pregnant. We were so excited. I began reading my Word more often and believing God for our son. I prayed over my womb daily and asked God to provide us with a healthy baby boy. I started studying specific scriptures of testimonies in the Bible of those who specifically prayed for sons and God answered. I believed strongly in my heart that *whatever* I asked for, God was sure to provide (Mark 11:24). Time went on and as it got closer to the time for us to find out the sex of the baby, I began to share my fears with my husband. I feared he would resent me if we had another girl, but my husband reassured me often that whether it was a boy or a girl he would remain the same.

The day finally came for us to find out the sex of our baby. Man, can I tell you my emotions were all over the place. As we walked to the back to the ultrasound room, I looked at my husband as he anxiously waited, and I smiled. The ultrasound technician asked if we would like to know the sex of the baby, and we both replied, "Yes."

She responded, "Congratulations, you're having a baby girl."

Shocked and struggling to fight back tears, I was crushed. My stomach was in knots, and the walls seemed to be closing in. A girl? "But how?" I asked myself. I tried to keep on a good face because I didn't want my feelings to trigger my husband. I couldn't even look at him. I felt like a failure. We walked to the car in silence. I didn't even know how to comfort myself, let alone give comforting remarks to my husband. Finally, I asked him, "Are you ok?" He replied, "I'm good but I ain't trying again."

His silence was deafening. It was truly the longest one-hour drive back home as I sat in that truck wondering, "What did I do wrong God?" "I prayed, I read your Word, I was faithful towards you!" "I believed in you, I trusted you and you ignored my plea."

The days following the ultrasound were hard. My loved ones were all asking about the sex of the baby. Every time I answered them, it was like reliving the experience over and over again. I would open my mouth to speak and would instantly feel sick to my stomach. Darkness became my comfort. Lying in bed became my security. Silence became my peace. Isolation became my best friend. "Faking it" became my mask of protection. Crying was just as constant as breathing. The more depressed I became, the more distant my husband and I became from one another, and the more detached I became from my pregnancy.

I remember telling one of my friends, "I don't want this baby." I had completely disassociated myself with my unborn child. It was truly a hurtful feeling not wanting her because she wasn't what I asked for, so

in turn this made me more depressed. I felt unworthy to be her mom because "How could a mother feel this way towards her child?" I thought.

Crippled with tears, anger, and frustration, I was angry with God for months because He had not come through for me. Have you ever prayed and asked God for something and He didn't answer? Have you ever believed God to bring you out of something and instead He allowed you to go through it?

Well sis, I've been there... I *was* there. All I could do was wait on God (Psalms 27:14). Prayer seemed distant to me, so I just talked to God like I would talk to my home girl. I remember asking God to forgive me for being ungrateful. I also remember telling Him how I was thankful for what He had done, even if it didn't go as I had planned. Then I remembered God's word in Isaiah 55:8-9, "My thoughts are not your thoughts, neither are your ways, My ways." Let me just shout right there. God allowed me to see two things. One, I put my trust in a baby to "fix" my marriage, instead of putting my trust in God to restore my marriage and two, His plans for my life were far greater than my plans for my life. ""For I know the plans I have for you," declares the LORD (Jeremiah 29:11)." Once I received that revelation sis, the enemy had to let me go. I began decreeing and declaring over my life and the life of my daughter. The enemy's plot was to destroy me and by default destroy my seed. Satan is after generations. I took power over my mind, and I declared power over my life and fought back with God's Word.

Dear Young Woman,

You have the power to change any situation, not because of who you are, but because of *whose* you are. Don't allow the enemy to convince you into believing otherwise.

Falicia McKarry is a proud wife to husband Martell McKarry and mother of their children. She is also a poet, speaker, and author. Falicia is a proud member of Full Life Faith Ministries. She is a graduate of Dillard University where she earned a Bachelor of Science in Nursing in May of 2015. Falicia is currently working as a mental health nurse while also pursuing her master's degree in nursing education.

Falicia founded *SIC & SAVED, which means SISTERS IN CHRIST who are Spiritual, Admirable, Virtuous, Elegant & Diligent on July 1, 2015.* Her ministry is devoted to the uplifting and spiritual development of women. Falicia enjoys using her gift of poetry to give testimony of how God delivered her from sex, drugs, alcohol, and other addictions. Her only mission in life is to die empty, by using all of her gifts while on Earth, and to hear her Father in Heaven say, "Well done my good and faithful servant!"

IG/FB: sicandsaved

Storms That Build

The sound of thunder followed by the quick flash of lightning that illuminated my room is what I chose to focus on, on this particular night. I sat straight up in my bed with my towel wrapped hair and looked at the TV. There was a faint blue glow in the room from the weather channel that was on at 2:47 am. I hadn't been asleep, just lying there listening to the storm and going over idle thoughts in my mind. I reached under my bed and pulled out the bottle of tequila that I had been drinking all day, and then a shot glass from my dresser drawer. I put on some socks (they happened to be a vibrant yellow), and for a second, I thought what a bright and happy color it was. A striking contrast to the moment I was in.

I took the bottle and shot glass with me into the kitchen, cut a lime into slices, and took it all with me in the bathroom to blow dry my hair. I remember locking the door behind me. This wasn't a part of my life that anyone had been privy to. I was the only one who knew this secret. I could still hear the thunder from the storm outside. As often as I heard thunder roar and lightning strike, I would take a shot and chase it with lime.

When I was done blow drying my hair, I put my things away and reached for the bottle that was on the counter. With everything fuzzy from intoxication, I accidentally knocked the bottle and a little handheld mirror off of the bar, and they crashed onto the hard, peached colored tile making the loud and very distinct sound that only glass can make when it is broken. I stared for a moment at the mess in a slight panic. My children were asleep in the next room, and I didn't want to wake them. There was also other family there with me that I didn't want to have to explain the smell of alcohol to. I started to cry. I got on my knees to clean it up and caught a glimpse of myself in one of the pieces of broken mirror.

Who was this person?

Did I recognize her at all?

Was this who I "had" to be?

So right there through tequila and tears, I made the choice to decide. I chose not to be the person I had become, and while on my knees surrounded by broken pieces, I asked God to help me with the broken pieces of my own life. I said to Him that this is what my life had become when I was unable to handle the pressures of life and relationships, and the demands and expectations that come with it.

As I began to pick up the broken pieces of glass and seemingly of my life, I realized that I indeed had help. That God was there with me, even in my darkest hour. That wasn't my last drunken night, but it was a defining moment that helped to guide me towards deliverance. I believed it was drinking that I needed deliverance from, but that was merely a manifestation of an underlying problem that needed to be dealt with. And God began to show me. Every fruit tree has seasons. When it is time, they bloom and produce fruit. You can pull the fruit off every season as it grows, but as long as the tree is still rooted, it will grow back. God was getting ready to begin showing me the root of the problem.

The Root

I am the youngest child of the two daughters my mother has and the middle child of my father's three. My parents divorced when I was very young, and while trying to figure out their own young lives, my sisters and I were sort of left to do the same. When a person doesn't feel important to anyone or validated by anything, it creates a void inside. The enemy is continually looking for a void to fill in our lives. We have to make sure that we leave no place for the devil to occupy. Literal things can be used to create doubt in us as well as things that aren't quite what they seem.

As a child I felt unimportant to my parents and the enemy used certain situations to deepen that erroneous feeling. I believe that every child needs the affirmation of their parents. They need to know that they are essential and that they matter. To affirm means to validate or confirm. Daughters need a special affirmation from their fathers. He is whether he wants to be or not her very first measure of a man. What he looks and thinks like, what he does and says or doesn't say, all have a very heavy bearing on ideals shaped in her mind. She needs to know from her father that she is of value, smart, and beautiful. She also needs to know that she is an asset. Without it, she will grow up with the inadvertent need for validation from someone, something, or somewhere else.

The most significant instance that I can recall as a child where I felt I was of no value to my father happened when I was ten or eleven years old. My sisters and I were getting ready to watch a movie with my dad (we had movie nights often), and while he was putting on the video, I picked up the case and noticed the duration of the movie in minutes on the front. I decided to muse out loud saying, "I wondered how long that was in hours and minutes." This quickly caught my dad's attention, and he became angry and aggressive, saying it was simple math and that I should know it. It wasn't that I didn't, I just felt the reaction diminished me because he shouldn't have acted that way about it if I didn't. I pretended a bit longer to see exactly how far he would go.

My older sister offered to answer because the tension had become so unbearable in the room, she seemed to want to help me, but he threatened her to silence her and me as well to answer. I did to save myself from whatever was next, but I never forgot that moment. There were many others, but that was the most significant. I didn't feel validated by him. I instead felt slighted. I had been yelled at and threatened because he thought I was unable to do simple mental math. That probably wasn't his intent, but the enemy used that space created in my mind to plant lies. "You're not smart, not beautiful, ultimately just not good enough." I became estranged from my father emotionally.

So, as a young teenager in my first relationship, I dealt with a lot of things that a person who knows who they are just would not deal with. Lying, cheating, physical, and verbal abuse. Because after all, he chose me, right? That had to mean I was of value because he wouldn't leave. When a daughter grows up without her father's affirmation or the wrong affirmation, she will take whatever affirmation "feels" right in that moment. I felt I was loved, so I stayed in a toxic relationship for ten years and had three children.

Looking back, I can see how God was always there though. Through one of my grandmother's kind words, or when I was younger, and I'd win a writing contest at school. God sent my best friend to me during my darkest season after we hadn't spoken for a very long time. I didn't even realize I was estranged, depressed, and drinking daily. We went to Bible study on a Wednesday night, and I was drunk on the front

row, yet no one knew. I remember the preacher saying "you are who God says you are, NOTHING LESS" that stayed with me. Because if God, who is the creator of all things thought that I mattered, what did man's fickle opinion of me mean?

The enemy will use whoever and whatever he can to try and tell you who you are or who you are not, but the truth is, only God can make that distinction. I came out of the hardest seasons of my life when I began to focus on the truth of God's word. It is the one constant in this very fluid world. It will never change.

The word says that my worth is far above that of rubies. That I am above only and not beneath, that I am royalty. I had to get the revelation that God is always present and that any situation we find ourselves in is subject to His authority.

We cannot choose where we come from or who we come from, we can only choose not to let it define us. I left that ten-year toxic relationship and didn't look back once. I know now that God is a father to the fatherless and a mother to the motherless and that He chose me. There is no greater honor than to be chosen by the CEO of all creation.

Dear Young Woman,

Hold your head high and know that your inheritance is rich. You're held in high esteem by the giver of every good and perfect thing. Begin to claim it even. That every good and perfect thing is yours through Christ. You are part of the ecclesia, a chosen priesthood through the death and resurrection of Christ Jesus. Your worth is far above that of rubies, and you ARE an asset. You have an assignment, and it is your responsibility to do whatever it takes to see it completed in the earth. No matter where you come from, remember that it is no determination on who you are. God is the only one who can make that call, and He thinks highly of you.

You were bought with a price, and it cost God everything to save your soul. Your value is limitless. When you recognize a pattern in relationships, anything contrary to what is good or pure or lovely, leave it. Begin to speak positive affirmations over your own life and watch God expound on them. Don't be afraid to access support; we grow through divine connections and learn from them. Also, don't accept negative words spoken over your life, your self-worth and self-image is yours to cultivate. Don't give anyone that kind of power over you. And most of all young woman, learn to walk in love. For love covers a multitude of sins. Doing these things will give God something to work with, leaving space for the miraculous in your life.

Rashunda Glenn is a 34-year-old mother of three, and a resident of Hammond Louisiana. She was born in Jacksonville, NC but raised in the state of Louisiana. She considers this southern domain her home.

She is a junior at Southeastern Louisiana University, majoring in Psychology, minoring in English with a concentration in creative writing. She hopes to become a Psychologist when she graduates. She loves writing, reading and learning new things. She is a freelance editor, and a poet. She believes she is called to women and is passionate about the issues they face and equipping every young woman with enough starter knowledge to cultivate who she is in Christ.

4

The Sunken Place

perator: 911, what's your emergency?

Caller: I'd like to report a suicide.

Operator: Who is the person, ma'am? What's their name?

Caller: It's me…

An empty prescription bottle lay next to a half-empty bottle of water. I walked over to my bed and lay down on my back. I closed my eyes and smiled. Soon it will be over. I won't feel all of this pain anymore. I hear the ambulance in the distance, but by the time the paramedics get here, it'll be too late.

By far, this was one of the darkest times of my life. I felt completely alone, like God had abandoned me. I could no longer make sense of my life. I had convinced myself that God couldn't possibly still love me, and that's why my life was going to hell in a handbasket. I had fallen into an alternative lifestyle and remained in a toxic relationship I knew I shouldn't have been in. I felt like everything was my fault and that I was getting exactly what I deserved. Life was happening to me at an alarming rate, and I'd lost my grip on everything I thought I'd been holding so well. I was barely eating, and I was sleeping all the time. I didn't want to see or speak to anyone. I was depressed.

Most days I didn't even make it to work, and if I did, I didn't say much to anyone. I would come home, take my prescription for my chronic migraines (even if I didn't need it), and sit in the dark, drinking wine, until I fell asleep. I would still call my mom at night and pretend that everything was ok, and my close friends just thought I was busy working a lot of overtime. I suffered in silence. I was terrified of being judged, and appearing weak and incapable of handling my problems, like I thought an adult was supposed to. The depression had completely overwhelmed me, unlike I've never felt before.

My circumstances broke my heart, and my spirit destroyed by life's relentless beating. I didn't want to deal with life anymore. I had convinced myself that everyone in my life would be better off without me. Still, I wondered if there was a better way to cope other than wine and self-medicating. I was tired of the mental anguish. I was in a deep, dark, sunken place, but I didn't really want to die, I just wanted the pain to stop.

Depression: What a taboo word in the African-American community. My whole life, I'd been taught an unhealthy suspicion of all health care professionals under the guise that all they wanted was money. I'd heard things like, "Shrinks are for crazy people, you must need crazy pills if you have to talk to the crazy people doctor, are you losing your mind? God is all you need, pray about it, and it will get better." And while the latter may be true, as Pastor J and First Lady J say, "God's sovereignty is always joined with human responsibility."

Talking to a "shrink" or going to a medical doctor was the most unnecessary thing to do, according to my dad, because "No one can tell you more about you than God, so pray about it and don't waste your money on foolishness." Up until now, I'd lived by his words. I lived by them even after being diagnosed with clinical depression at fifteen years old after my first suicide attempt (yes, that part). I was in search of answers that would help make my pain go away and so I thought about it, "Why would God put these health care professionals in position if I wasn't supposed to use them?" I've heard more times than I can count, "In order to get something you've never gotten, you've got to do something you've never done." I know right, cliché. But this little saying helped me take the most significant step of my life, and so against everything I'd ever been taught, I called into the employee assistance program through my job and made an appointment to speak with a counselor.

I no longer cared about what anyone else thought about mental health counseling or what they would think about me if they found out I was seeing a "shrink." I was hurting so badly. Every day I felt myself slipping deeper and deeper into that painful bleak abyss. I was afraid of

where I'd end up. I finally admitted that I not only needed help, but that I wanted help, and it was the best decision I have ever made.

I met with Ms. Jay for six weeks, and I'd never before been clearer in my thought processes. This encounter even helped me develop my relationship with God. One of the things I worked on in counseling was the unconditional love and acceptance of myself. The more I began to grow in self-love, the more I began to seek God. I've come to believe that self-love, care, and stewardship over your health (mentally, physically, and spiritually) and finances are an act of worship to God. What better way to show my love and adoration to God than to take care of myself and the things He has given me? I also realized that it is up to me to seek out the things that will grow and mature me in a well-balanced, healthy, and fulfilling lifestyle. Once I learned to love myself and accept myself unconditionally, I no longer entertained things or people who threatened my peace of mind. I learned how to say no, and how to set safe boundaries so that I could operate at my fullest potential. My relationship with God is stronger, and I am living life now and not just existing.

Dear Young Woman,

Sis, breathe. It's ok NOT to be ok. It's ok NOT to always be strong, to NOT always get it right, and most importantly, it's ok to ask for help when you need it without feeling shame, guilt, or judgment. Don't be afraid to reach out for help from a mental health professional, a pastor, or a trusted friend or mentor. As selfish as this may sound, love and unconditionally accept yourself and take care of you FIRST because you cannot pour from an empty vessel. If you are not operating at 100%, then it won't be possible for you to give sufficiently and efficiently in any other area of your life. Put your self-care as a priority and not as just an option.

**Mechelle Pollard** is a woman of God and a 32-year-old single mother to a beautiful baby girl named Kyla. Mechelle is a woman walking in purpose. By trade, she is a federal security officer with the Department of Homeland Security but knows her God given purpose as a healer to help women and young girls walk in alignment with Godly purpose.

As she fulfills her purpose, she is pursuing a master's degree in Clinical Mental Health Counseling from Walden University Online, planning to one day open her own counseling center to be a healing light to the community where she was raised. She is an active, as well as a member on the praise and worship team at her church, Triumphant Church of Luling, La. Her life's purpose is to be a catalyst for healing in others by sharing her story.

Too Desperate for Love

When I met my ex-husband, I was twenty-two years old. I was a single mother of one, and still dealing with the disappointment that things hadn't worked out between my son's father and me. I was living with my godmother temporarily to save up enough money to get an apartment of my own. I met "Dee" in the neighborhood where I lived because his mother lived a few houses down the street from my godmother's house and we would see each other often. I must admit, I wasn't interested in him at all, but he was very persistent in pursuing me. He would send messages through my friends, and my godmother would even tell me that he asked about me. I laughed it off every time.

One particular night, I felt like getting out of the house, but none of my friends were available to go with me. So I got dressed up and decided to be bold and hit the club by myself. I often look back on that night and wish I had stayed at home because this is where it all began.

I sat at the bar for a little while and had a drink. I stood around the dance floor and watched everyone dance and have a good time for about an hour; then I was ready to leave. As I walked out to my car, I never noticed that someone was following me. Dee walked up behind me and asked for my telephone number. He tried to spit a little game at me, but as I said before, I wasn't feeling him. His cocky attitude intrigued me a little bit, so I listened and laughed as he talked. He then took out a big wad of twenty-dollar bills and told me to write my number on one of the bills. I thought to myself, "Since he wants to flash his money to impress me, I'm going to get as much as I can then leave him."

I'm sorry to say that is not how the story ended. We began to see each other often, and he always made sure to include my son when we went places together. That is what ultimately softened my heart towards him. He showed attention and concern for my son when his own father wasn't doing that. That is where I should have been more careful because a man will come along and show you the things that he knows you are longing for just to get you in deep. If you have any weaknesses or insecurities, a man who has bad intentions knows exactly how to lure you in and get you on their hook. Well, I was the big silly fish that bit the bait.

I wish I could tell you that I didn't see his cheating, lying, and emotionally abusive ways before I married him, but the truth is I saw it all, and I thought marriage would flip some magical switch in him and make him change into the man that I needed him to be. Unfortunately, his behavior got worse after the wedding because he knew it would be much more difficult for me to leave him. I wanted so desperately to have the two-parent household for my children that I didn't have as a child, but I realize now that desperation had blinded me. I put up with women calling, texting, and leaving voicemails. Women were coming to my job to pick fights with me. He would come home with passion marks on his neck, and some nights he wouldn't come back at all.

Several times I caught him with my own eyes at another woman's house. He had two kids with his ex while we were married. One night, his ex-girlfriend and her sister showed up to my house to fight me. I could literally go on and on about my experiences with him. I became obsessed with catching him cheating and lying because no matter what evidence I found, he would deny it. I was going crazy and living in a constant state of paranoia. I felt something terrible was going to happen if I didn't get away from this man. I had reached a breaking point. I begged him to just leave and let me go through the pain of being alone and healing myself. He taunted me saying that he was never going to leave me, and I was never going to leave him. I began to fantasize about harming him physically, and I told him this. He just laughed in my face. The feeling of hopelessness that he created in me had become heavy, but I was too scared and weak to leave on my own. I wanted him to leave me so I would have no other choice but to move on. I never told my friends or family about what I was going through because I wanted to maintain the image that we were good and happy.

He tried to turn me against my friends, telling me that they were no good and that if they had the chance, they would be with him too. I realize now that it was all coming from his insecurities. An insecure man will try to make you feel low and make you believe that he's the only person that cares about you. Sadly, I believed this for many years. We had two more kids together during our marriage, so as a mother of three boys and I thought to myself, "If I don't stay with this man, what other man is going to want me with three kids?" I'm here to tell you today that there are plenty of men out there who will love a woman with three kids or more and treat you like royalty. I know this personally.

A valuable lesson I learned from this experience is that we teach people how to treat us by what we accept. I must admit that I didn't know that I deserved better and I didn't believe that I could find it. When a man knows that you love him, and he mistreats you because he knows you will stay, that is called emotional abuse. In my broken way of thinking, I believed everything that happened was just a part of the "ups and downs of a relationship." It's sad that as young women we are taught that the more pain you take from a man, shows how much you really love him. A man who truly loves you would never test your limits in that way. I thank God that he brought me out stronger and wiser.

Dear Young Woman,

Please love yourself enough to walk away from anybody who doesn't love you enough not to hurt you.

Erica Warren is a first-time author and a former customer service agent in the banking industry who now works independently educating and empowering families to build wealth in their local communities. She is especially passionate about reaching the younger generation and giving them a head start in the money game.

Erica was born and raised in a small town called Franklinton, La until the age of 18 when she moved to Hammond, La to attend college at SLU. She lives in Hammond now where her four teenage sons were born and also reside. She loves inspiring and encouraging women to be confident, fearless and to go after their dreams in life.

To learn more about this author you can follow her on Instagram @e_class100 or on Facebook @Erica Warren (Eclass)

6

Blindsided

"And they overcame him by the blood of the Lamb, and by the word of their testimony..." (Revelation 12:11)

Between the ages of six and eight, I was molested by my mother's boyfriend. It always happened when I woke up from a nap and used the restroom. I learned to hold my urine as long as I could in hopes that my mother would come home, so I could go to the bathroom without him bothering me. Funny, that just popped into my head while I am writing this. To this day, I have to remind myself to go to the bathroom because I don't think about it. He always said it was our secret and not to tell anyone, but I told my mom and my stepfather when I was twenty-one or twenty-two.

At the time, I did not realize I had suppressed the whole ordeal and that it would manifest in different parts of my life. I did not find older men attractive. I hated when people hugged me without me initiating it. I never really understood why. More manifestations came out when I became sexually active. I was "smart" about who I gave my body to for moments of "pleasure." It was a game for me. I would study the guy I wanted, flirt, bait him, and keep him dangling for a while until I was ready to sleep with him.

I always kept the same guys around, so my body count would not go up, or at least that's what I told myself. All the while I was still in church, putting on my "Sunday Best" because I mean, I have needs, right? Once every seven to eight months was okay because at least I'm not like this person over here who sleeps with anyone. At least, I'm "smart." I was smart until I ran up against the one who broke me. I knew he wasn't the one for me, but I fell in love with him. He was my first love. I had a boyfriend in college, and I did love him, but this guy, I was IN love with him.

It wasn't until September of 2017 when I had an encounter with Jesus, and He showed me myself. I had been saved since the age of twelve years old. I rededicated my life to the Lord in my twenties, but I didn't really start living for the Lord until September 2018 when I was thirty-two years old. I laid my life down at Jesus' feet, and that's when everything opened up for me. The Lord showed me that this game I had been playing with men was a defense mechanism I had developed. I truly believed for the longest time that all men wanted was sex, so I would give them what they wanted so I wouldn't have to build a relationship. I was afraid of relationships. Although my mouth would say, "I want to get married," and "I want to be in a relationship," my heart was saying the opposite.

I thought I was ahead of the game. I thought I had everything mapped out precisely, but as much as I had studied and watched the mistakes of others and planned a different way for myself, I was still getting played by the greatest mastermind in history, Satan. He blindsided me, and I had no clue. I prided myself on how smart I was until I ended up getting played, but I thank Jesus Christ for His grace. I don't want to think of where I would be if it had not been for Jesus stepping into my life when He did.

On that Saturday morning in September, I sat on my bedroom floor and wept uncontrollably. I felt the Lord's presence in such a marvelous way I had never felt before. It was like He filled my room with Himself. I had never felt love like that before. It was overwhelming. The Lord spoke to me and told me that I had so much buried inside me that no one could see it, not even myself, but He knew it was there. He continued to tell me that He couldn't send me my husband until all of that was out of me because if He would have sent Him before I would have messed him up.

Wow! I still cry when I think of that encounter with the Lord. It was almost like Paul's encounter with the Lord on the road to Damascus. I'm not the Apostle Paul, but I do believe we all have a moment like that in our lives, a moment that is a turning point for us in our Christian walk.

I pray that my testimony touches someone's heart. The scripture I referenced above is so true. I have overcome by the blood of the Lamb and the word of my testimony. It is uncomfortable, but I know someone needs to hear it.

I pray that through the pain I've gone through, someone is made free through Jesus. I pray the Lord uses my words to reach those who are hurting or lost. I pray that if there is a young woman who has been abused that she does not give up hope. Seek help. Find a counselor, a pastor, someone who will listen. I pray that the Lord sends someone to help you out of the situation you are in right now. The Lord WILL turn it all around for your good. I pray that you break free of the chains holding you in the name of Jesus Christ, Amen.

Dear Young Woman,

Your past does not define you. You are more than what happened to you in your past. Yes, you may have gone through horrific experiences, but you are still living and breathing today. You may question the goodness of the Lord through all of the things you have gone through, but just know what you went through may help someone to break free.

Stephanie Cooper resides in Southeast Georgia where she was born and raised. She currently works as a special education teacher in the public school system. Stephanie dabbles in photography when she is not educating the minds of young children. She is heavily involved in her church where she handles the music for praise and worship among many other things. Stephanie loves the Lord, her family, and close friends. She plans to continue writing to encourage and strengthen women in their walk with the Lord. She hopes that her testimony can shed the Light of Jesus to those hurting in the darkness.

Broken into Beautiful

The biggest culprit throughout my life has been rejection. It makes sense that the enemy uses rejection to make us feel abandoned. Rejection opens up the door for so many thoughts to enter our minds. After dealing with rejection in my childhood, I was always looking for love in all the wrong places. Even though I had grown up in church and always had a relationship with God, He was just God to me, He wasn't yet "Father." My internal need for intimacy was expressed through my external need for physical pleasure. I needed to feel close. At the same time, I felt like the more I pleased others, the more they would want and accept me.

All I really wanted was to feel loved. I wanted someone to tell me that I was beautiful. I thought that the more I gave of myself, dressed seductively, and accepted whatever treatment they gave me, I would then be accepted enough to be loved. I didn't realize that I didn't love myself and that I was waiting for someone else to make me feel like I was worth loving. I tried to be everything and do everything that a man wanted just so that he would love me. I didn't realize that in trying to be everything, I had no idea who I was.

Because I had no idea who I was, it was easy for men to come and go after I was no longer of use to them or after I had annoyed them enough with my clinginess and desire to be around them every second of the day. When I wasn't with a man, I felt completely empty and alone. Being rejected by men and at the same time not being happy with my own body because of the years I endured being teased in grade school for being flat-chested and not having a big butt; I began to lust after women. I secretly wished that certain body parts looked like someone else's. That desire to look like other women eventually became the desire to want to be with them secretly. I didn't realize that the molestation and rejection in my childhood had opened the door to sexual perversion. So, after going through a divorce and then dating men who were no good for me, my lust for women was heightened.

Rejection always opens the door for lust and sexual perversion. My desire for women was heightened even more after I was rejected once again by a man. This time I decided to act on my desires and become like what had rejected me for so long going back to childhood. I asked a friend, who I knew entertained the homosexual lifestyle, the same friend I always ministered to about God, to come over to my house.

After flirting with her on the phone, she came over, and I continued to flirt with her. I kissed her and wanted to take it further, but she stopped me and said, "No, just preach to me Tera!" Those words almost choked the very life out of me. Not only was I rejected once again, but I also felt like I couldn't even fulfill a desire that I thought was going to satisfy the longing in my soul.

After this incident, the Lord showed me that I was repeating a broken cycle because of my lack of intimacy issues that I never dealt with, and that had affected me in my childhood. The Lord wanted to heal all of that pain, but I had to give it to Him. I had to forgive those who just didn't know how to love me properly. I had to forgive those who I felt rejected me. I had to forgive myself for the decisions I made out of brokenness. I had to open my heart once again and be vulnerable to receive.

God showed me that no person could ever be everything that I needed them to be, and to place that much responsibility on another person was unfair. God showed me that He was the only lover of my soul. He is my center of joy and peace, and without that understanding, I would continue to attract those who didn't know how to properly love me because I'd showed them that anything they gave me would do because I lacked joy and peace within.

Once again, I turned to God because I needed another layer of healing, where I had to let Him come in and be the lover of my soul and not allow my thoughts and desires to rule. I had to let Him show me where those thoughts and desires came from. God showed me the root of those desires was rejection and not being confident in who He created me to be. My addiction to pornography, thoughts of homosexuality, acts of fornication, adultery, masturbation, low self-esteem, depression, and being a perfectionist were all rooted in rejection, verbal and emotional abuse, and molestation from my childhood! I had to give all of that pain to Him and let Him heal me and reshape my mind.

When we heal through an intimate relationship with God as Father, it removes the pain. The memory will never fade, but the pain of the memory can go because the Father comes in and fills every void. I love the Japanese technique, Kintsugi. It is a technique for repairing broken pottery with seams of precious metals, usually gold. The broken places are highlighted in ways that bring more exceptional beauty to the piece than would be possible without the break. It treats breakage and repair as part of the history of an object, rather than something to disguise. It is always the enemy's goal to get us to hide our pain and run from our past. The Father is saying, "Give all of it to me, so that I can fill in every crack, every broken piece, and restore it to a place of wholeness, and then let the whole world see so that they can see My glory through your life!"

Dear Young Woman,

Embrace every mistake and face everything in your past that hurt you. Forgive yourself and those who hurt you, so that you can be free from the pain and let God turn what's broken into something beautiful.

 **Tera Young** is an author, speaker, and transformational coach with a passion to help others embrace the fullness of who God has created them to be by healing from their past, breaking from free limiting mindsets, and being confident in their uniqueness. She has also mentored ex-offenders, youth, and women and helped individuals embrace their uniqueness by understanding what's in them that causes them not to know their true identity.

Tera has created several empowerment workshops that have been utilized at schools and organizations alike. Tera is currently launching a ministry that will minister to the hearts of women from the heart of God called "Broken Into Beautiful Ministries" through biblical counseling, coaching, speaking, and the performing arts. Tera's own testimony of being set free from rejection through intimate relationship with God through Jesus will minister to the hearts and minds of many.

8

Lost and Found

I had met the man of my dreams, Malcolm. He was kind, sweet, and easy on the eyes. He made me feel like I was the only girl in the world. We would go out on dates, hang out with family and friends, and just vibe with each other. I had several people tell me, "Girl, you need to leave him," but I just figured they were hating on me and jealous. He wasn't like anyone I had dated before, so within the first six months, I was already head over heels. Then things went south.

One night, I pulled up to his house. I suspected he was cheating, so I confronted him. He got so angry that he punched me in the face. I was devastated because here I am, just trying to have your back, and you hit me. I remember feeling so embarrassed. I stayed at his house for three days. He told me how sorry he was and that he would never do it again. I believed him, felt his remorse, and stayed. For the next few months, things were great. I had a child by him and thought that now we would be a family. He was a great dad, but not a great man to me. I wanted so desperately to have a family that I accepted the abuse. If I went out with my friends, it was a fight. It became so bad that I just cut myself off from everyone. I would go places and pretend everything was ok when deep down inside I was hurting.

Birthdays are an important part of the year for some. My thirtieth birthday was special because I was leaving my twenties, so I had a small party at my house with all of my closest friends. We had a blast that night. By this time, I had been in a relationship with Malcolm for about seven years. Malcolm was the jealous type and was a ticking time bomb, always ready to explode. I thought I knew how to handle him, but I was wrong. After my party, I walked over to my cousin's house. Her husband's brother was there visiting, so I stayed a bit, but not that long because I knew Malcolm would be home any minute and I had to get back.

Once I walked in the door, the arguing started. Malcolm was upset and accused me of being intimate with another man. He started going through my phone and questioning me about everything he saw. As I tried to take my phone from him, he picked me up and thumped me on my hardwood floors like a sumo wrestler! I literally saw stars. I got up and lunged towards him, hitting him with all my might. I was looking for an escape.

My cousin was in walking distance from my house, so I kept thinking that if I could just get to her house, I would live to see another day. I ran to the bedroom in hopes to lock the door and get out the window, but he beat me to the door. I ran to the front door. He came behind me, pushed me out of the way, and double-locked it. I took off to the back door with no luck. He was stronger than me. At that very moment, I felt like giving up. I was in a situation where I could not win. Here it was, my thirtieth birthday, and I'm ending it by fighting with someone who is supposed to love me. I was so tired of fighting. I was mentally, physically, and emotionally exhausted.

After realizing the game was over, and I was not going to win, I just gave in. I laid with him that night and was sweet as pie for the next couple of months. My birthday was on January 26, 2014. I used the remainder of the month to develop an exit plan. I knew that if I told him I was leaving, then he would start an argument, and one of us would end up dead or in jail. I had been in this toxic relationship for years, so I knew that it was just going to continue unless I made a change.

I prayed that God would lead me in the right direction, and then I reached out for help from a family member that was more than 500 miles away. In March, I drove a moving truck with my car in tow to Dallas, Texas, alone. It was the scariest trip of my life, and I cried all the way there. That first year I was so homesick and ready to move back. I had left my entire family behind without knowing what would lie ahead.

I was afraid that I would be in Dallas and fall back into the same strongholds that had held me down in Louisiana. I didn't know who I was, nor did I have a vision of what I wanted out of life. I took the year off from dating and focused on getting to know my likes and dislikes. I figured out what I was willing to accept from a partner, and most importantly, I learned how to love me. This was the most important lesson because I needed to learn how to love myself.

A lot of people who have never experienced domestic violence have a lot to say about what they would do if they were ever in the situation. The truth is you don't know what you would or wouldn't do if you felt your life was in danger every day. Holding it inside every day and pretending you are okay is not living. I had to take control of my life and know that my mind is the most beautiful part of my body.

Exactly one year after moving to Dallas and working on myself, I met my husband. He has shown me how to truly feel like a woman. He is the complete opposite of men I usually dated. He showed me how to communicate effectively and how to face my fears. We met in February of 2015 and married in June of 2015. My husband knew what he wanted, and he wanted me to know he was serious.

Dear Young Woman,

All is not lost. Rebuilding after you have lost everything, including yourself, takes time and focus. It is so easy to fall into old habits and feel trapped due to familiarity. Create a plan for your life and stick to it. Surround yourself with positive people who want to excel in life. Most importantly, you have to want to excel for yourself. No one can block your blessings and what God has for you, but YOU!

**Chasity Jackson-Watkins** is a 35-year-old native of Independence, LA. She currently resides in Dallas, TX with her husband Jackson Watkins and their girls Chelsea and Londyn. Chasity has been a lover of books and writing from young age. Chasity has provided a listening ear to many young women over the past decade. Her testimony of overcoming domestic violence and self-hate will inspire you to learn your value and know your worth. Chasity can be contacted via email at chasityj22@gmail.com, payhip.com/ChasityJacksonWatkins, or Facebook Chasity Jackson-Watkins, Author.

9

Protective Custody

There was a time when I started looking for love in all the wrong places. Because of my "daddy issues", I went from man to man trying to fill the void of being loved. I never gave myself time to heal, and that was not a good thing. Not one of those men was available to me when I needed them the most. Two relationships in particular totally drained me and left me tired. I was tired of giving myself away to men. No one was genuinely committing to me, so something had to give. I was tired of disappointing God. It wasn't enough for me to practice abstinence because my mind and thoughts had to be pure as well. The act starts in the mind, and as the Bible tells us in Proverbs 23:7, "As a man thinketh in his heart, so is he."

This last experience gave me the HUGE lesson I needed. I dated this guy years ago, who I thought I loved at the time. He came into my life at a very trying time and when I was vulnerable after losing my son. I would do anything for him and would try to help him in any way I could. And you know what? I did just that. I helped him whenever I could. After dating for a little over a year, I found out he had still been seeing someone else. I confronted him about it on two different occasions, and each time he persuaded me that he wasn't and even got mad at me for bringing it up. For the life of me, I couldn't understand why…lol.

All the signs were there, but I ignored them because I wanted to be with him. I was hoping he would change so that we could build something. As time went on, I just couldn't do it anymore, so I broke up with him. Fast forward some years later, and he jumped in my DM's, flirting, and asked to take me out. With little to no hesitation, I immediately replied and agreed to go out with him. He started off texting often and even sent something to me to my job and all of that. I thought that maybe this time would be different. Ha, yeah, right!

I used to think I had it going on because all of my exes would always return to me or at least try to return. Whew! That was so far from the truth. The truth is they came back because I was open and available. You teach people how to treat you. What you allow is what will continue, and as long as I left that door open, they would continue to walk through it. I allowed myself to continue being with him knowing he was still involved and thought it was okay because they weren't married. How dumb was I to make myself believe that I was doing no wrong?

Listen, it doesn't matter if he or she is married or not. If that person is involved with someone else, then they are OFF LIMITS. I realized that if the shoe were on the other foot, I wouldn't want someone to do that to me. As a matter of fact, it has been done to me, and I didn't like it. One day out the blue I received a message from someone telling me that he supposedly had an incurable STD and they thought I should know. Can you imagine getting a message like that about someone you've been intimate with and cared so much for?

All sorts of things went through my mind. I was so hurt. I questioned, "How could this be happening to me? What if it was worse than what she said he has? What if I have what she said he has? What if it was HIV/AIDS?" I was so angry, hurt, and disappointed in myself. I was already diagnosing myself with negative thinking and I hadn't even seen a doctor yet. This is sort of like what we do in everyday life.

We automatically start thinking the worse and speak negative things over our life. Just because a situation looks bad, doesn't mean that it is. It's important that we speak not only positive things over our life, but things that we want to see manifested as well. Needless to say, after testing and waiting for the results, I discovered that "I DID NOT HAVE A DISEASE!" I was so thankful, but this was a huge eye-opener for me. After this incident, I vowed to live fully for God and surrender ALL! I decided I was going to be celibate and remain pure. I'd tried this before, but this time was different. I wanted to truly live how God wanted me to live, to please Him and reap the many blessings He has in store for me.

In doing this, I needed to watch what I listened to, entertained, and who I was around. When you're living outside the will of God and having premarital sex, you attract soul ties, and they are real. The transferring of energies from who that person has been with before you can mess you up. Whatever spirit he or she has can attach itself to you and have you feeling depressed, drained, or even worse, suicidal.

Many of the relationships I had been in had me not caring about certain things, and it came in between my relationship with God. No, I don't blame them. I blamed myself for allowing myself to be in something that wasn't beneficial to me. For one, we were unequally yoked. None of them went to church, and we never talked about God or the future. My commitment, dedication, and relationship with God fell off. I didn't care about skipping church or any of that. All of my standards and beliefs went out of the window. I found myself "COMPROMISING FOR COMPANY!"

Dear Young Woman,

You do not have to compromise to receive love. Keep your standards high even if you get lonely. Don't allow the spirit of lust to have dominion over you.

 **Abreail Foreman** is an awesome woman of God, minister, and mother who has allowed God to transform her life in an amazing way. Abreail has endured many heartbreaking tragedies but allowed her pain to birth her purpose.

After experiencing the horrific loss of two children and being involved in previous toxic relationships, she became passionate about helping women. She specifically focuses on encouraging women who have experienced child loss. She also enjoys encouraging single women not to settle, to believe that they deserve better, love themselves first, and to wait on Gods best.

Through depression, anger, brokenness, resentment, and three suicide attempts, God has brought her out stronger than ever. Abreail is a living testament of what God can and will do. She is now walking boldly in her purpose and cheerfully serves the kingdom of God.

10

You Are Valuable

For the most part, I've been able to accomplish much of what I've set my mind to. I figured that since I've always envisioned being a mother, becoming one wouldn't be difficult once we started trying. Sure enough, the test was positive. Yes, I'm pregnant! I immediately began to think about the journey ahead. All sorts of questions ran through my mind, along with the feeling of excitement and fear.

I went on like this for a few weeks until that cold December night, when I felt the sharpest pain I had ever felt in my life. I eventually went back to sleep until the pain came again, which was followed up by a lot of bleeding. I knew enough to know that this wasn't normal. I still couldn't wrap my mind around the fact that something was wrong. This wasn't a part of the plan, and with all of the thoughts that were running through my mind, something going wrong was never one of them. As I drove myself to the emergency room, I told myself that although the situation was a bit abnormal, everything would still be fine... until it wasn't. The doctor told me I suffered a miscarriage. What I had prayed for, what I thought was going to be the missing piece to my life's puzzle was gone.

After this happened, I started to research. How many women does this happen to? What did I do wrong for this to happen? Maybe I waited too long to start trying. All sorts of thoughts about what I didn't do correctly for this to happen, started going through my head. Well after finding out that first time miscarriages are somewhat common, I figured it was just a fluke in my body, and I shouldn't have anything to worry about. I had to fix this. I thought my value as a woman was on the line. So, without processing the loss and without healing from it, I thought we should try again.

And try again, we did… and again, and again, and again. A few years went by, doctor's visits, cycle charting, medications, ultrasounds, changing my workload to support traveling back and forth to another state for treatment – these were just a few of our somewhat desperate attempts at a successful pregnancy and birth. We prayed and believed. We read the books, searched the websites, downloaded the apps, and asked the questions. I must admit, I was a bit stressed, tired, and discouraged. I didn't feel like a wife, a woman, or anything I once identified with. I just felt "less than."

After some years and tears, the pregnancy test was finally positive! I was happy, but I couldn't get excited, as I started thinking about all the things that could go wrong. I began to reflect on what the doctors told us, the fact that I'm a few years older than the first loss. But things were starting to look up as the weeks rolled along, and I let my guard down! As I'm looking at the ultrasound screen in excitement, I noticed that what I saw didn't look like the photos on the app, the videos, or in the books.

As I sat in disbelief, I heard the words, "Mr. and Mrs. Johnson, I don't believe that this pregnancy is viable." We left our appointment, hearing the strong heartbeats of babies through the other treatment room walls, as we walked down the hall. Heartbroken and angry does not begin to describe that feeling. I thought this was the cruelest joke in the world.

The grief I experienced was something that I didn't think I would get over. I was totally numb to the people and things around me. The only thing that I could feel was failure. I believed that I completely failed myself, my husband, and the legacy of my family. I was angry with myself, my physicians, and I even had the nerve to be upset with God. I was in serious emotional and physical pain. While in the hospital, I found myself questioning my worth once again. I returned to that "less than" invaluable place.

Let me share with you what I learned from this situation. I now know that my value isn't wrapped in society's timeframe, the proverbial biological clock, or any pressure from myself or outside influences. I no longer allow those painstaking "When are the babies coming?" or "What are y'all waiting on?!" questions to bother me. (Although, I just really wish people would not ask these questions at any time!) While I

am grateful for my husband, family, career, education, accolades, etc., those things hold very little weight when measuring my value. My value, my identity comes from my creator, God, as we all are created in His image.

Once I truly grasped that, my perspective on life suddenly changed. I decided to refocus my energy on things that facilitated my healing and kept me in constant reminder of my worth: worship and prayer, spending time with my family, and volunteering my time to help others were just a few things. I knew that in addition to taking the time to heal physically, I also had to heal emotionally – to really just process the anger, disappointment, and the confusion that plagued my mind.

Do I still shed tears sometimes? Absolutely. Do I still believe that my husband and I will be parents one day? Without a doubt. Do I question, "Why me"? Most definitely. But what if for no other reason, these experiences that made me feel so invaluable were not only for me to understand how valuable I am, but more so for me to be able to share these lessons with you?

Dear Young Woman,

We all face circumstances that may lead us to question our value. You may not be facing my exact situation, but maybe you didn't make the team you tried out for, someone you really liked decided that they didn't feel the same, or maybe your parents aren't showing you the attention that you may be needing at this time. My advice to you is this: know that you are valuable. We are all hand made by God for a purpose. Whatever situation you are facing that is causing you to question your value as a young woman, as a person, as God's masterpiece, please understand who and whose you are!

YOU ARE VALUABLE!

Love, light, peace, and tranquility to you.

 **Cherie Johnson** doesn't consider herself an author; however, penning her most recent experience to contribute to this project sparked from her desire to encourage others.

A recent Dillard University "40 Under 40 Alumni Honoree", Cherie utilized skills gained from her career in Human Resources, to create "Your Seat at the Table" - a women's career support service. Cherie has been a guest speaker for various empowerment events and helped to launch the Gr8 Table Talk podcast, which she periodically co-hosts. In her community, she is an active member of the Triumphant Church, Delta Sigma Theta Sorority, Inc., and is also a volunteer with Dress for Success. Cherie is a lover of the arts and enjoys being with family and friends. She is happily married to Mark Johnson Jr. and they reside in their home state of Louisiana.

To connect with Cherie, please visit www.yourseatatthetablellc.com or follow @yourseatatthetable on Instagram.

11

Against the Grain

I became sexually active at the age of twelve years old. It wasn't because I was "fast" or "curious," but simply because I was looking for validation from anyone who would provide it. It just so happens that a handsome young man told me that I was pretty. That one word changed my mindset and caused me to do many things that I'd later regret. I became pregnant with my first child at the age of fifteen.

After twenty-four weeks of pregnancy, I began to experience complications. I went into preterm labor and my worst nightmare became my reality. My daughter was in the NICU (neonatal intensive care unit) for fifteen days. On Saturday, November 27, 1999, I received a call from the doctor advising my family and I to come to the hospital as soon as possible. They explained that they had done all they could do for my daughter. As her organs continued to fail, I was faced with a major decision. I had to decide if I was going to let them resuscitate her or if I was going to allow them to pull the plug. Imagine being fifteen years old, having to decide to take your first child off of life support. It was truly one of the most traumatic, life altering experiences ever. I chose to let them pull the plug…

A few months later, at the age of sixteen, I became pregnant again. I carried my daughter for five months, and then I began to experience pre-term labor, yet again. I couldn't believe this was happening to me! Shortly after arriving at the hospital, I gave birth to my daughter. However, she was stillborn. My entire world was flipped upside down. There I was, sixteen years old, burying my second child. I suffered from severe depression, paranoia, and suicidal thoughts. I just wanted to die. Thoughts of continuing life after losing two children was almost unbearable. However, something inside would let me commit suicide, although I desperately needed an escape from life. I needed to change my life because clearly, it was not going in the right direction.

After losing my children, I found God. I decided to give my life to Christ and I really wanted to live as holy as possible, but there was one problem, I wasn't ready to stop fornicating. You see, sex was a crutch for me. I would have sex whenever I was bored, lonely, craved attention, or I needed to feel "needed." Even though I loved God and wanted to do what was right, I wasn't ready to stop doing my thing.

At the age of seventeen, I became pregnant again and gave birth to my son a few months after graduating from high school. I had big plans to move to another city, start college, and begin living my best life. The father of my child decided to leave, so I had no choice but to become a single parent. This definitely wasn't part of my plan, but I had to adjust.

It was rough! I still lived at home with my parents. My son was premature, so he was unable to go to a daycare center due to his immune system not being fully developed. If he had gotten sick, it could have been fatal. I was unable to work, so I had to apply for welfare. I remember my monthly welfare check was $188. That was my only source of income for about a year.

I applied for a college that provided single parent housing. I was so happy when I got approved and was able to move on campus and start college even though I had an infant. I also applied for food stamps, which I used to buy formula because WIC didn't cover the special formula he needed. Thankfully, a family friend agreed to watch my son free of charge while I attended classes.

It was a rough season, but I can honestly say God was with us through it all. I still don't know how we made it on $188 a month, but little is much in the hands of our God. Things were going well, but then life happened. My son got sick and was rushed to the hospital. He was diagnosed with pneumonia and was hospitalized for almost a week. Needless to say, I was a wreck.

Due to him being in the hospital, I was unable to attend classes, which caused me to fail that semester, but I didn't care because I was more concerned with the health of my child. I dropped out of college and had to move back in with my parents. I felt like a complete failure. All

I ever wanted to do was defy the odds and beat the statistics that say that most single mothers are stuck on welfare and dependent on the government for assistance. However, at that moment I felt like I was the poster child for African American single mothers.

I heard that the parish was accepting applications for section 8 vouchers. I didn't want to live dependent on government housing but living with my parents wasn't an option either. I camped out all night long in the line to make sure I was able to submit my application. Once I made it inside, I was greeted with a grimace from the intake worker. She spoke to all of the applicants like we were trash. I felt even more like a failure, but I pushed past those feelings because I had a son to think about.

Shortly after, I received a letter stating that I was approved for a voucher. My son and I were able to move into a newly built 3-bedroom, 2-bathroom house in a beautiful subdivision. I re-enrolled in college and graduated with honors three years later.

After graduating from college, I wrote a letter to the housing authority to thank them for the voucher but told them that I no longer needed it. My goal was to use government assistance as a stepping-stone, not a stumbling block. I used it to finish school, and then I began a career to better take care of my son and I.

I worked several different jobs but never found fulfillment or a paycheck to cover our expenses. I knew that I was called to entrepreneurship, but I was afraid to step out. I couldn't handle failing and having to live with family members again, so I kept a job, that is, until I got fired. The day I got fired was one of the best days of my life. They thought they were hurting me when they fired me, but honestly, they freed me. I took a leap of faith and started a business. Now I have two businesses that allow me to operate in my God-given purpose on a daily basis. I spend my time serving God, pursuing purpose, and pushing others into their purpose.

Dear Young Woman,

It doesn't matter where you started or what you have experienced. God has a well thought out plan for your life. His Word reminds us that all things work together for the good, so it doesn't matter how bad it may seem today. Your past doesn't dictate your future. You are destined for greatness, and you must know that better than you know your first name. If God can take me, a little country girl who was pregnant three times before my eighteenth birthday and mold me into a world changer, guess what boo, He can do the same for you!

Alandria Lloyd is a serial entrepreneur, self-published author, and certified personal development life coach. She is the author of:

- *Change AGENT: The Missing Piece*
- *Fasting for Change Prayer Journal,*
- *While I'm Waiting Devotional for Single Women.*
- *Letters to My Future King*
- *Girl Power Uncensored (co-author)*

Alandria is the owner of a book publishing company, The Writer's Block LLC. The Writer's Block assists aspiring authors by teaching them how to write their books in record breaking speed and become published authors without breaking the bank. She offers online writing classes, book consultations, book coaching cohorts, publishing packages, and more.

Alandria tries to encourage everyone she meets to share their testimonies in the form of a book. She has suffered many trials but has found solace in sharing her stories within the pages of her books. She is a living, breathing testament that God will give beauty for ashes. Alandria resides in Hammond, La with her teenage son. She lives life on purpose and is determined to fulfill her God-given destiny.

To connect with her, please visit her website bit.ly/TheWritersBlock or send an email to info@thewritersblockllc.com

You Are Worthy of God's Best

In high school, my love life was nothing short of tragic. Either a guy that I didn't like, liked me, or I liked a guy, but he didn't like me. A friend of mine once told me that if I ever wanted a boyfriend, I should lower my standards because they were way too high. I didn't listen, but little did I realize that my standards weren't high enough, and I eventually fell in love with a BIG MISTAKE.

After high school, I started dating a guy who I thought met all of my standards. He was a Christian, went to church, and was a virgin who wanted to save sex for marriage. I fell hard for him very quickly, and it seemed as though he fell just as hard for me.

As our relationship progressed, we started getting really serious. After only a few months of dating, and despite wanting to wait until marriage, he pushed the physical boundaries, and I allowed him. Within five months of our relationship, I was no longer a virgin. We had unprotected sex again a couple more times after that. After each time, I went to the pharmacy to purchase Plan B because he didn't think I should be on birth control since we weren't going to have sex anymore. I asked him to come with me for support, and he refused, citing that he knew too many people and didn't want someone from church to see him. He also didn't want me to tell my mom.

My mom had wanted me to wait until marriage but told me that if for any reason I chose not to, to come to her first, and she would make sure I was taken care of. Despite this, my boyfriend said that there was no need to tell my mom since we weren't planning to have sex anymore. The thing is, we kept having sex. So, when I eventually told my mother, he became very upset with me. Our relationship started to fall apart, and he blamed it all on me.

The relationship went back and forth, and as it continued, it became more emotionally and psychologically abusive and toxic. He became more narcissistic and only wanted me around when it served him. He continued to seduce me and push the physical boundaries, and each time after we had sex, he would make me feel guilty and say that we weren't being "good Christians." But if I ever turned him down, he would make me feel guilty about that too, and say that I didn't love him or he would withhold any affection, even kissing, hugging, and holding hands.

Once I would have enough of his behavior, he would cry and tell me how depressed he was and that he was thinking about his dad's gun that was in the other room. Eventually, I would end up crying, apologizing, and trying to convince him to stay with me. This was how every conflict ended.

This went on for two years, causing destruction to my relationship with my parents, friends, and even to myself, and my emotional and spiritual well-being. I started to think that I was asking for too much in the relationship.

Once I started seeing the truth, I knew that I shouldn't stay, but I didn't feel worthy enough to be in a better relationship after giving myself away so easily.

When he finally used me as much as he wanted and decided that he no longer wanted me, we broke up, and I felt like I had lost everything about myself. I lost the chances of making my dream of going to England a reality, I left a wreckage of bad grades and reputations with professors, and I was in the worst depression I had ever experienced.

I knew God had called me to be a wife one day, so I continued to pray for my future husband, but I didn't feel like I was worthy of the good man I was praying for. I cried out to God one night and told Him that I wanted Him to heal me, protect me, and keep me from falling in love again until he introduced me to my husband. And God did just that. As I waited for God to introduce me to my husband, I spent all my time with God, and He worked on healing my pain and mending my broken heart.

He introduced me to inspiring Christian women at my church, online, and brought in old friends that comforted, supported, and ministered to me during my time of healing. I never felt so close to God as I did then. As I became closer to Him, I discovered who I was again and whose I was. I rededicated myself and my purity to God, and I decided to wait on God's best for me. Now, I am happily married to God's best for me, and my husband is taking me to England at the end of this year so I can finally live my dream.

Dear Young Woman,

I know that you really desire a relationship, but don't ever settle. When I tell you that the man God has for you is worth the wait, he truly is. Your friends and the rest of the world may tell you that you should lower your standards but don't. Instead, raise them. Expect nothing less than God's best. And just because he goes to church and says he's a Christian, doesn't mean he's God's best for you. Pay attention to what he does, not what he says. Does he walk the walk? Or is he all talk?

Expect a man to love you the way Christ loves you. Christ does not tear down, threaten, do or say hurtful things, manipulate, or withhold affection. And neither would God's best. Every man you date, place his name in place of the word "love" in 1 Corinthians 13:4-7, and ask yourself if each statement is true about him. If not, then he doesn't know what love really is. Lovely, if you are in a toxic relationship, break it off and immediately surround yourself with support and prayer, because leaving a toxic relationship is difficult, and you can't do it alone.

If you've made a mistake, and have a soul-tie with someone, it's okay. You are NOT worthless. There is forgiveness, grace, and love at the cross, and Christ paid the ultimate price for you. You are VALUABLE and WORTHY. Never let the enemy or anyone else make you believe otherwise.

Amanda Davis is a loving wife, faith blogger, writer, librarian, and most importantly - a follower of Jesus Christ. Married to her Once in a Lifetime love, Timothy, God created their beautiful love story back in 2012, and were married in April 2015. They have two beautiful cats, Artemis and Tabby, and reside in Greenville, Texas.

Amanda loves God with all her heart, and her deepest desire is to inspire others to love Him as well. God is using Amanda's past pain to help reveal to young women that they are valuable, have worth in Jesus Christ and to wait for God's best for them in their lives.

If you want to read her full testimony and are interested in reading more from her blog, you can visit her website at www.butterfliesinmytea.com or follow her on the following social networks:

www.facebook.com/butterfliesinmytea.com
www.pinterest.com/btrfliesinmytea
Twitter: @btrfliesinmytea
Instagram: Butterfliesinmytea
You can also contact Amanda at amanda.butterfliesinmytea@gmail.com

13

Bruised, Shattered, Broken, but Blessed...

When I was in my early twenties, I met my ex through a mutual friend. I was a single mom, just looking for love. After a few months, we started dating. In the beginning, things were great. He made me feel special and wanted. He did nice things for me that no other man had ever done. But then, after we had been dating for about a year, the verbal abuse started. We had gotten into a disagreement about something. He became furious and called me a lot of names, and then pushed me against the wall.

Even though I was fussing back with him, I became scared when he pushed me. I began crying and asking him why he had done that. He apologized and said he was sorry and would never do it again, but that I had made him mad.

This was the beginning of years of physical and emotional abuse. We would get into such bad disagreements that he would always threaten to hit me or make me feel worthless. He would take my keys to my car if I tried to leave and would always throw in my face what he was doing or had done for me.

When the disagreements became physical, he would always buy me a beautiful gift or give me money and apologize. I was so insecure and dumbfounded that I always accepted his apologies and told myself that he was having a bad day or that maybe if I would be quiet and do like he said, things would be better. He always made me feel like no one else would want me because when I met him, I had a two-year-old daughter.

In 1999, I became pregnant and didn't even know it until I had a miscarriage. I was devastated. I know I had that miscarriage because of all the stress and fighting. In 2000, I became pregnant again and had my second child, a boy. This was my ex's first child, so I felt that since I was giving him a child, things would get better. But once again, I was dumbfounded. It seemed like the verbal, mental, and physical abuse got that much worse. When I was about eight months pregnant with my son, my ex and I got into a big disagreement that went bad. I remember just like it was yesterday. He began to fuss about something and really got upset with me, and whenever he would become angry, he would literally turn into someone different. He began to push and shove me. I tried to fight back, but he was so much stronger than me. I remember us fighting from inside the house to outside in my front yard. I was screaming and crying, just asking him to stop. I even threatened to call his uncle or his cousin. Sometimes, if I couldn't get him to stop, I could call them, and they would either come over or talk to him on the phone.

He grabbed ahold to my hand and bent my fingers back. It brought me to my knees. He was so angry that he just kept on bending my hand. I was crying and asking him to stop because I was eight months pregnant, but he didn't care. I experienced so many different types of abuse with my ex, but the incident that changed me forever happened after we got married.

After dating for five years, and having his son, we got married. We fussed and fought up until our wedding date. We got married on a Saturday and left that Sunday on our way to Florida for our one-week honeymoon. I was sick the day we got married. I thought I was catching a virus or something, but now I realize it was God warning me one last time not to get married.

When we got to Florida and checked into our hotel, I was really feeling bad. All I wanted to do was go to sleep, but my ex wanted to have sex, and I just couldn't. He began to get so angry, so we started fussing. Things didn't go well. I went to grab my cell phone to call my mom, and he snatched it away from me, and started choking and hitting me. I was so scared, and in that very moment I just wanted to die. I felt that was the only way for me to break free. I couldn't believe this was happening to me on my honeymoon. But like always, he said he was sorry and took me shopping.

I felt that my situation would never get better and that this life would kill me. I said to myself, "He will never let me leave him. January 2015, my life changed. What the devil meant for evil, God turned it for my good. What I thought was going to take me out, ended up saving my life. My ex had been arrested.

I decided enough was enough when he became incarcerated. In that time frame, I realized how much my life was worth, and that God had a plan for me. It didn't matter what I had done; God was still waiting for me. Seeing how different and happy my children were, gave me the strength to walk away and provide them with a life of love and peace.

At first, it was very hard to leave. I felt guilty, and like I owed him something, but with the prayers of my mom, I realized I wanted better, and God would give me everything I needed. I started to feel loved again, but most importantly, I felt that God had answered my prayers, and I had been forgiven. I finally was free after nine years.

From this experience, I learned several things. I learned that we should always listen to God and that you can never change a person that doesn't want to change. I learned to never look for a man, but instead to let him find you and to make sure he is sent from God. I also learned that being silent is not the answer. I believe it was my silence that made the abuse continue for many years.

Dear Young Woman,

You must believe in yourself and know that you deserve better. Abuse doesn't get better if you do nothing; it keeps getting worse. Love doesn't hurt. I know it's hard, but you can get out, you don't have to live like this. Love and forgive yourself; you deserve better.

Demetria L. Baker is the founder and president of Refuge of Hope, Incorporated, a 501 3 (C) non-profit organization located in Rustburg, Virginia. Demetria is also the CEO, at Lynchburg Municipal Employee's Federal Credit Union, located in Lynchburg, Virginia.

Demetria has been married to Lewis M. Baker for the last 7 1/2 years. Demetria has two children, a daughter named De'Nitria (22), and son named Tyvon (18). Demetria has currently been in the ministry for 5 1/2 years and is an ordained minister. Demetria enjoys spending time with her family, doing outreach, and community service. You can follow me on Facebook, at Demetria L Baker, and Refuge of Hope.

Instagram dlbaker2u.

Releasing What Once Held Me Emotionally Captive

Many times, negative thoughts become our obstacle or emotional chain of bondage that blocks us and keeps us from obtaining true happiness and spiritual growth. We stagnate in negativity. We continue to load up on a roller coaster of emotional anger and bitterness, shutting down on the people we love and those that try to love us. I have experienced emotional bondage where I trained myself to think it wasn't a problem, but in essence, it was a prodigious problem. My emotional bondage affected the way I related to others. It also affected the way I handled relationships and hindered my ability to trust and find the good in people.

As a young girl, I was sexually abused by a teacher on a school field trip. I remember that day, that time, that feeling, and those fears of mistrust. I held the pain of that day for a long time. Nobody knew how I felt. I went to counseling two times, and everyone thought that

was the end of the public story, but no one acknowledged the fact that a story was still being told on the inside. I was angry, bitter, hurt, and disappointed until one day in 2010, which was twenty-two years later. I was driving to work and almost lost control of my vehicle at the red light because I was so deep in thought. I said, "God, I forgive him." Immediately the burden was lifted, and I began to experience internal peace. God told me that it was no longer my story; it was His story. He freed me that day, and I was able to make peace with my past.

I disconnected myself from the pain. I stopped thinking about it, stopped replaying it in my head, and I stopped committing an injustice against myself. I allowed my wounds to close. I started to see that my future was so much brighter than my past. God had something for me to do, and He was not going to allow me to ruin what He had created and the plans He had made. Forgiveness is real, and it is essential for our spiritual growth.

Unforgiveness is much more than a simple thought or mere feeling that one carries around day to day. The thoughts of resentment, anger, hatred, and harm can lead to actions that we will be sorry about after the fact. I chose to no longer allow these thoughts to linger and occupy space in my head. Once I made this choice, I was able to experience peace. When I chose to forgive it wasn't about others, it was about me. I was set free. In order for God to forgive us, we must be willing to forgive others and ourselves. I know it can be hard, but it's not optional, it is a requirement. I was able to do it only because I believe in God, and I believe in His word. Galatians 5:1 says, "Stand fast therefore in the liberty wherewith Christ hath made us free and be not entangled again with the yoke of bondage."

I started to tell myself positive stories as I lay in the bed at night. I started standing in the mirror every morning telling myself my own "I AM's" as I went out to the face the world. I began feeling better every day. I am not going to lie to you, it was a process, but it was a process that was made possible through God. I told myself that although things that I did not like or ask for had happened to me, they were no longer in my physical reality and therefore it was not going to be allowed in my mind. God is bigger, and He was so much better than anything I could have thought of. I no longer had to feel the way I had been feeling.

This story in my life was just one scene of what can be viewed as a play of my life, and it had a short role to play. Some characters are killed early on in a play and they're never seen again. This part of life had played in the scene it was scheduled to play in, and now it had to go. I had to embrace the bad and move on to the next act in my life. I got connected to God. I began to reconnect to my spirit. I made a vow to myself, and there's nothing like making and keeping an agreement with yourself. God helped me to start pursuing life and pursuing it abundantly.

I learned to embrace the life that I had left and refused to go to sleep another day angry. I refuse to allow yesterday's hurts and pain to be invited into my sleep and in my time of peace and freedom. I would tell myself I am an overcomer, I am a survivor, and I am not a victim.

I am at peace with my past. I will not allow anything or anyone to stop what God has started. When God created me, He already had a purpose for me. He didn't make me then have to find something for me to do. God already had a plan, and my life was planned from the end to beginning from day one.

I learned to let go and let God. I stopped dominating with my forcefulness and began flowing like the waters in a river's stream. I began to flow everywhere there was an opening. I began to experience the flow of freedom in my life. I started to write, read, and travel. I began to heal. I begin to picture myself being soft, feeble, resilient, and gaining access in places that I was once excluded from because of my preference to be non-resilient and tough. I thought I had to protect myself. God didn't need me to do what He does. I gave it all over to Him, and every day, I learn how amazing He is. I decided to let it all go, to live, and to fully trust God. I am now an action taker that walks daily by faith.

Dear Young Woman,

I know God will tell you just like He told me, "Daughter, I got you." When His whisper hit my spirit, I knew that I would never be bound again. The same goes for you. That same freedom is obtainable for you. Trust Him.

Dr. Onika L. Shirley, the founder and CEO of Action Speaks Volume, Inc. is an International Confidence and Procrastination Coach and Motivational Speaker. She is a Christian Counselor. She is the former President of the Greater Memphis Chapter of NAPW for almost 5 years. Dr. O is the Founder and Director of Action Speaks Volume Orphanage Home in India and Founder and Director of Action Speaks Volume Sewing School in Pakistan.

She is a ten times author, master storyteller, radio host of Action Takers Walking by Faith Live radio broadcast, and serial entrepreneur. Dr. O is a mother and proud grandmother to baby Aubrey which is her everything. Of all things Dr. O does, she is most proud of her profound faith in Christ and her opportunity to serve the body of Christ.

Contact information
actionspeaksvolume@gmail.com

Website:
http://actionspeaksvolum.com/

Instagram: https://www.instagram.com/actionspeaksvolume
Facebook: https://m.facebook.com/actionspeaksvolume/
Periscope is actionspeaksvo2
Twitter: http://www.twitter.com/@actionspeaksvo2

15

Don't Lose Your Way

"We don't ever talk about you, and we don't bring you up. There is no residue of your presence in his life." These were the words spoken to me, by the woman that my daughter's father was seeing; as we both tried to plead our case for a man, we both loved. After hearing these words, I took my focus off of being a single mom to seven children, one of which was a newborn. I no longer focused on the newness of my baby girl and embracing being a mommy again.

Even though it didn't make sense, I wanted to become "residue." I wanted her to see my dirty clothes in his bed and my jewelry on his dresser. And even though I still entertained having a very physical relationship, I couldn't seem to smear enough of me on to him to catch her attention. I wanted to be the "residue" that she saw and questioned him about. I wanted to be the one that caused the arguments that would eventually draw him back to me. I wanted her to feel my

presence every time she was with him. I tried to make her believe that he, at one point, was interested in me, even if it was only for a few minutes.

For the first few weeks of our daughter's life, I was constantly reminded that I never had a relationship with him and that we may never have a relationship outside of raising our daughter. I replayed the very intimate moment we had shared in my head for weeks. It plagued my mind that our extremely short meeting had led to me being vulnerable and easily undressed. I had responded to my body instead of responding to my spirit. My heart was extremely wounded, to the point that I could feel the pain penetrate whenever I thought about him, said his name, or saw him. This man that I had only known for forty-eight hours and had given my body to, was a complete stranger. I allowed him to take possession of my body, and I allowed him to be intimate with me without any protection.

Our brief encounter would have a lifetime effect on both of our lives. For the first time in a long time, I became blind. I felt like I had lost my way. I lost myself with the thought of not being "the residue" that she could see. I lost myself trying to become the woman that I thought he would want to be around. I lost myself in trying to be the woman that put the spark in his eyes, the one that he couldn't stop thinking about and the one that he couldn't imagine his life without. I wanted to be her! More than anything, I wanted to be the one that he wanted. The more I tried to become who I thought he wanted; the more my soul became tied to his. When things didn't pan out the way that I planned, I was left with my thoughts, and my thoughts paralyzed my actions. My soul was tied to this man, yet he rejected me. To him, I was just sex and a pretty smile.

I remember being very active in ministry. As a matter of fact, I was a leader in my local church, and I was sold out for Jesus! I was ripping and running from meeting to meeting, outreach, and providing service to the community, and was finishing my second discipleship class, and I was preparing for discipleship graduation. It all came to a screeching halt the morning I found myself pregnant with my seventh child. I was scared and unsure of what I was going to do next. My dignity ultimately left me, and the small amount of self-confidence and self-esteem I had, suddenly disappeared.

My heart ached days at a time, and I just wanted it to stop. I just wanted to wake up and not think about him or her, and what they were doing and why he had chosen her. I thought about what they were talking about and laughing at. I even thought about what they ate. I thought about their business transactions. I became consumed with a life that I was not a part of, one that I wasn't even invited to. I felt like dying would feel better than the heartache I was experiencing.

I needed to refocus, and that meant that I had to stop thinking of myself so negatively. I didn't know that casting down the very thoughts that held me captive, would be the very thing that set me free. I started by forgiving myself for the encounter that led to me becoming pregnant. And then I began to "dig." I began to dig my well in the Word of God. I meditated on Psalm 84:1-11 and I would dig and dig

and dig into the promises of God. I began to refer to every verse as if God Himself was speaking directly to me! I started to believe what I was reading, and then I began to speak positive words over myself. I called myself SET APART and CHOSEN, and I believed it!

Dear Young Woman,

I encourage you to stay focused and not to lose sight of your destiny. Don't lose yourself chasing something or trying to become someone that God didn't call you to be. Don't lose yourself because you aren't sure what your value is. Take the time you need to pour into yourself and let God love on you. Stay true to you despite your current situation. Dig your well by diving into the Word of God. Look yourself in the mirror and confirm that no one can ever be you, or do you, like you.

 **Schemeka Bowrin** is a generational curse breaker! She is a single mom to seven children, blogger, aspiring motivational speaker, and published author. When life didn't have a seat at the table for her, she created her own table. Schemeka is the CEO and founder of The WriteHER Connection, an organization that mentors and speaks to the heart of young girls and women. Which creates a no-judgment zone, safe space, and allows them to tell their story.

Schemeka has faced numerous adversities in life from abusive and toxic relationships, being her own worst enemy, and a toxic mommy. She has battled alcohol addiction and suffered the trauma surrounding abortion. However, each time life knocked her down, she got up even stronger.

Despite life's harsh treatment, Schemeka chooses to live and walk graciously with the confidence that she is blessed beyond measure. "My story could have been written totally different."

16

Love Yourself and Know Your Worth

There was a time in my life when I didn't know who I was, nor did I know my worth. I have always struggled with my identity in the spirit as well as in the natural. I have always settled for less than I deserved because I didn't make wise choices in my life. I am sharing my story, as a testimony to a young woman, in hopes that you will make wiser choices in life.

As long as I can remember, I have longed to be loved by prince charming. I used to read love poems and watch love stories and dream of one day being swept off my feet by my knight in shining armor. Well, one day, I met my first husband. Mutual friends introduced us, and we seemed to have hit it off right away. We had not known each other very long, but I was in such a hurry to begin my dream life that we got married at the courthouse and moved in together. Shortly after we got married, he quit his job, and I was carrying the weight of all the bills

alone. He always lied about looking for a job. Unknown to me, he was having an affair with the neighbor who lived in the apartment downstairs. That explains why she never liked me.

His demeanor changed, and he became very mean and abusive. He didn't want me to see or talk to any of my friends. He became very controlling and tried to isolate me from everyone. He used to accuse me of cheating with the garbage man, the mailman, and any man that looked my way. It was to the point that I couldn't speak to any of my male friends because he was so jealous and insecure.

One day one of my female friends came to see me because no one had seen me in a while. I was a very social person, so it was unusual for me to not talk to anyone. My husband was going out with some of his friends, so she came to see me. She told me that she was afraid for me and that she was there for me if I needed anyone to talk to. About an hour later, my husband came home, and my friend was still there. It was evident that my husband had been drinking. You could smell the alcohol on his breath, so my friend decided to leave, and I walked her out to the car. She and I were standing on the porch, of the apartments, and we were talking and laughing about old times. We hugged each other and made plans to see each other again soon.

I watched her leave in her car, and I walked back up the spiral staircase to my apartment. As soon as I stepped into the apartment and closed the door, I felt a sharp pain across my face, and I fell to the ground. I felt another acute pain across my face, back, and stomach. When I realized what was happening to me, my husband was punching me in the face and kicking me in the back, abdomen, and anywhere he could kick. I could feel the warm blood run down my cheek, as I tried to cover my face and stomach. I could feel my face and eyes swelling up. I managed to ask him what is going on and he told me that he overheard my friend and me plotting to meet some guys. He thought that my friend was trying to set me up with a man. He continued to abuse me physically and verbally while I lay on the floor in a fetal position.

He finally got tired and walked away from me. By the grace of God, I got a second wind and the strength to get up and run out of the front door, and down the spiral steps. I know I hit those spiral steps two at a time because he was on my heels running after me. I ran out of that front door like a gazelle running for her life. When I made it to the parking lot, I started screaming for help as I ran for my life.

As I screamed, the neighbors turned on the lights and came outside to see what the commotion was about. My husband stopped chasing me, but I kept running until I reached the front door of my friend's apartment across the parking lot. She buzzed me in, and I called the local police and my parents to come to get me. That night I left my husband, went to the hospital and pressed charges against him. The next day I broke the apartment lease, moved out of the apartment, got a restraining order, and filed for a divorce. I never looked back, and since then, I've been living my best life. I'm a single woman in my fifties, and I love it. I'm trusting God to send me a mighty man of God, but until then, I'm working on my dreams while serving the kingdom of God.

DEAR YOUNG WOMAN

Dear Young Woman,

Learn to love you and don't be in such a hurry to find love. Fall in love with God first, then fall in love with yourself. Learn your likes and dislikes, explore new things, think outside the box. Get to know you and spend time alone with yourself. Take yourself to the movies and dinner. You are worth it. Know your worth.

Don't settle for less because you are lonely. Be happy with yourself. Discover your purpose and use your talents and gifts to serve the Kingdom of God and help others. You don't need a man to validate you because God approved you before you were in your mother's womb. You are worthy. God already loves you, unconditionally.

Be bold and courageous and travel the world to discover new and exciting things that you never thought you would do. Don't settle for less than you deserve because God wants us to have His very best. When God sees that you are ready love will find you. Until then, be patient and seek God and learn to love God's presence and yourself. In doing so, you will discover your purpose, and everything will fall into place.

 **Evangelane Turner** is a well-educated woman of God with a big heart for others. She holds a Bachelor's in Social Services along with a Master's in Leadership.

She is a seasoned, licensed minister and faith-based counselor, Evangelane has led several support groups in areas such as grief and recovery, marital healing and family restoration. She is the founder of Heart to Heart Ministries, Inc., but mentoring in a singles ministry has allowed her to unleash her fun side.

Facebook: Evangelane Turner
Email: evangelane.turner@gmail.com

17

The Secret She Kept

I'm the middle child of five children. I can't recall when or how my mom met my baby sister's dad, but I can remember how nice he was to us. I also don't recall my momma being pregnant, but I do remember her bringing my baby sister home. She named her after her daddy, whose name was Ken, but everyone called him Kasey. Eventually, we went from country living to city slicking where parades would pass right in front of our door. We would stand on the balcony and watch the huge, colorful floats roll by while screaming, "throw me something mister." Kasey was the father I never had. We were a family. But then something happened.

The sexual abuse, which I believed was "tickling" at the time, started before I turned five. He made it seem as if it was a playful thing, so I thought it was ok. I remember one morning my mom went to do some laundry, and she left us at home in bed with him. I can never forget him grabbing my little foot and rubbing it against something that felt weird. Later in life, I realized that it had been his penis. One night my mom and Kasey passed words, about what, I don't know, but I can still see my mom destroying almost everything in that house. She broke lamps, dishes, televisions, and even cut up the furniture. That same night my cousin picked us up from our old corner house in Algiers, and just like that we were on our way back to live with granny with no hesitation or explanation.

When we moved back to the country, it was time for me to start kindergarten. I excelled in school, and I was on the honor roll every nine weeks. I was content with life at that moment. Well, would you believe that in the midst of my happiness, he returned? I don't recall any abuse this time. However, I vividly remember him beating my momma unmercifully. There had been a family get together full of all kinds of food and excessive drinking.

Later that night, after everyone had left, things took a turn for the worse. First, it was the loud shouting and disrespectful profanity. Before I knew it, my momma was falling down the steps with my baby sister in her hands. He threw blow after blow as my mom struggled to fight back. She must have landed a good one because he grabbed a broomstick and started beating her with it. After snapping out of a state of shock, I ran as fast as I could while screaming for help. My aunt and I returned to find my mother lying on the ground, beaten, almost unconscious. She was rushed to the hospital, and he went to jail. I can still see her bloody, broken, and bruised. Some images never leave you.

About four years later, right before my fourth-grade year, he came back around in a nice ride with a bunch of promises. I was nine when my momma asked me what I thought about her taking him back. I wanted to say, "Momma don't do it, please!", but those words just wouldn't come out. I suppose I was afraid she would ask me why. I was nine with blossoming breasts and thighs thicker than most of my peers. The abuse became way more aggressive. Now instead of "tickling" on top of my clothes, he would fondle underneath them.

The feeling of fear, shame, and confusion hit me like a ton of bricks after the first time, the hard skin of his hands touched my private parts. I felt as if it was my fault. I wondered, "Why me?" I didn't understand. I believed that if I told, my mom would kill him and go to prison, so I kept my mouth shut and avoided him as much as possible. My sisters and I needed our momma, and that's all I could think about.

The more my body matured, the more I hated it. I hated to even wear clothes that showed my shape in any way because he would respond with sexual slurs. I tried my hardest not to look good around him, hoping that maybe that would stop him from looking at me or trying to touch me.

My insecurities were at an all-time high, and I was uncomfortable in my own skin. I played all kinds of sports and did all types of extra curriculum activities so that I could stay out of the house. He died when I was fifteen. I stood in front of the church, crying my eyes out as I read his obituary. After the funeral, everyone asked me if I was alright. They could never imagine how relieved I was that he was gone. I felt free and safe. I didn't tell my mother about the abuse until I was thirty years old. I kept that secret inside, and it did more harm to me than ever. He was dead, but his memory was very much alive.

I buried my pain, and it grew roots. Self-sabotage began. I tried to sex it away, smoke it away, prescription pill pop it away, party it away, work it away, spend it away, and more. Those were just bandages, bandages that I had to tear off and give the wound air to heal. The healing process began once I spoke my truth to my mom. I started seeking God more by fasting and praying. Personal development, self-care, and self-love became very important to me. Writing positive self-talk on my bathroom mirror, exercise routines, and inspirational videos also helped. I also began seeing a professional counselor.

Healing is a hard process, and that's why you have to work at it continuously. I give my insecurities, negative self -talk, and trust issues a name when they come to discourage me. I call its name and tell it to flee. I'm not just surviving anymore; I'm thriving.

Dear Young Woman,

If you've had a similar experience, I challenge you to dig deep inside of yourself and find the courage to speak your truth sooner than later. You don't have to carry the burden alone. Seek God first, and then professional help. God still loves you. You're worthy. You're deserving of good things to happen to and for you. Don't allow your pain to break you. Use your pain as your power to push through. Yes, pain changes you, but we have the choice of what kind of change we allow. Good or bad. Choose wisely.

 **Estelle Taylor** was born on November 5, 1986. She is the third of five children, and as the middle child, she has always been the strong, independent type. Most of Estelle's young life revolved around church, writing poetry, and reading. Estelle graduated from Boothville-Venice High School where she was a Beta member and also student council president. After high school, she attended The University of Louisiana at Lafayette, where she majored in psychology.

Estelle is a 1st-time author and poetry lover. She is the mother of two young kings, and she is also the owner of the online boutique, "Lady Lituation Boutique." Most know her as the goofy lady that makes everyone laugh, but there's so much more depth to her. She is finally ready to use her experiences to help others heal with her words of wisdom and FEARLESS LOVE!

*THERE IS NO FEAR IN LOVE
1 John 4:18

18

The Love That Taught Me Self Love

They say you have three great loves in your lifetime. The first is puppy love- young, idealistic, fairytale love. The second teaches you valuable life lessons that stay with you forever. It's the love that hurts. And the third is the love that sneaks up on you. It's the one that will make you thank God that the other two never worked out. My first love was cool, as a matter of fact, we're still cool. The third I'm still praying about. Lol... But honey, my second love? My second love is why you're reading this. My story started back in 2006. I was a recent college dropout with no plan, who had just had a miscarriage.

The summer had come to an end, and I guess my stepmom got tired of seeing me sitting around with nothing on my mind but getting cute and having fun with my friends, so she went into operation "You need a J.O.B." mode. My uncle worked at a local grocery store, and we

knew he would hire me. I was hired within forty-eight hours and was ready for work. I started working and walked right past love number two. He was working, and I was late for work. Later he would tell me that he asked me how I was doing, but I kept walking. From my point of view, my uncle had told me that if I was late, I was fired. So my goal was to be there on time and to collect those checks every week!

Not long after this, number two and I started dating. We went out every weekend to dinner, the movies, and whatever fun we could think of. I always heard that the best way to get over a man was to get under another one, so I decided to love hard. I loved him harder than hard. I wanted him to know that when he saw me, all he saw was LOVE. Love would get us through ANYTHING! He had never been in a long-term relationship, and he really didn't have a great example of what a healthy marriage looked like, but I was ready to love away anything negative he ever thought about love.

So I allowed years of disrespect, hurt, anger, frustration, and more because I just knew that if I stayed a little longer and showed him that I was down for him, he would step up and marry me. I mean, who wouldn't want to marry me?

I was just getting my life together, we had a child, and we were one big happy family. My daughter was a joy, and I just knew the more I showered him with love and affection that he would see my efforts and repay me with a ring.

Little did I know I was wasting my time by forcing someone to love me instead of loving myself. I was so far gone that I didn't even recognize myself anymore. I was just existing and surviving. I remember one day I took him out to this popular hibachi spot for his birthday, and I had invited family and friends. I was wearing a diamond ring on my left-hand finger, and his friend said, "I didn't know you and Tiara were engaged." I heard him say, "Oh, we not engaged." I was so hurt by his tone. To me, it sounded like he was saying, "The audacity of his friend to ask him that as if he would ever marry me."

I took the disrespect a few more years. I even thought he was all I deserved. I can recall a time when I tried to take my life because I thought my child would be better off with someone else to raise her. I literally lay in the tub one day and cried out to God hysterically, begging, and pleading that if he would keep me and help me get my life together, I would forever praise Him.

As the years flew past, I began to find my morals, values, and worth again. Sometimes we as women don't know that we don't have to deal with someone until someone else shows us what we deserve. I started to develop a genuine and intimate relationship with God. It wasn't easy at first. I tried my way for the longest time, but what I love about God is how patient He is. He allowed me to go through some things, and He showed me how to love myself all over again. God is such a gentleman.

As I started to believe in myself again, and God began opening doors for me, my faith grew. The more my faith in God increased, the more

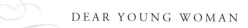

my need for a man decreased. The need for me to find my purpose in who I was, had become vital. I remember listening to number two tell me I couldn't afford rent on my own every time I would say I was leaving him. He would say your lifestyle and your bills don't mix; you need me. And I believed him. I even stayed an additional two years.

Eventually, the time came where I had become so in love with myself, that one day I packed my stuff and left. I prayed to God to help me get out of a situation that I thought I couldn't get myself out of. I had acted out in my flesh long enough, and for me, it was time to act in my faith. Within those two years, I had grown stronger, and I started to believe in myself. I began to walk in stride again. I began to walk and talk like a queen, act like a queen, and move like a queen. My dreams got bigger, and my depression got smaller. That walk began to hit different because I knew who I was and whose I was. I was a woman in love with God and myself. I began to understand that no matter what I go through, God would always be my side, no matter what.

Dear Young Woman,

If I could give you any advice, I would say never to forget who you are. You are a queen, you are worth the wait, and you deserve to be treated with respect. If a man can't give you that, then you can't give him the time of day. Don't ever think you can change a man. Change yourself, the situation, and the direction of your life from a waste of time to worthiness from God.

**Tiara Johnson** is a serial, pure-bred, entrepreneur, and mom boss! She is a native of Washington DC where she raises her 11-year-old daughter, the future Madame President 2048. She is the Founder and CEO of "Women with Vision," "Her Seat at the Table," and "Styled by Tiara J," where she assists women bosses in training. She helps them to find their purpose, as well as take the necessary first steps in launching their brands and businesses.

Tiara's organizations are founded on love, support, unity, and women's empowerment. Her mission is to empower today's woman to reach greater heights for tomorrow's world. Tiara also is a freelance wardrobe stylist where she pledges to make the everyday woman look like she is walking straight off the runway. Her favorite quote is "When you believe in yourself, other people will believe in you too."

Indestructible Woman of Grace

The heart of a loving woman is indestructible. Women of faith can move mountains, and women who open their hearts to love after being hurt repeatedly are the bravest. I applaud myself and other broken women who pick up broken pieces and move on with their lives. For those that haven't found their true potential, I pray that I can enlighten your dark spaces with hope because a woman with faith aims for better days.

At one point in my life, I felt like all men were disgusting! The fact that I was raped at age nine, molested when I was eleven, beaten at seventeen, and almost dead by twenty-two puts me in a unique position. I could have lost hope, but in every situation, what others saw as a burden, became my blessings in the form of another life. Suicide attempts failed me twice as a child. I gave birth to two beautiful children while going through post-traumatic stress and domestic violence.

There wasn't a day that I did not fear never being able to see my children again.

Being abused as a child, I was told to lie to get my mother out of jail. I was raped and didn't know it. I carried that pain daily. Although I did not understand what happened, I knew it was wrong, and it hurt.

First, I approached my mother in the tub, "What does it mean when you bleed?"

"Are you bleeding?" she asked. "Yes," I replied.

"Oh, you starting your period," asked my mother.

I sat on the toilet and asked, "What if I can't pee?"

"I'm gone take you to the doctor," she answered apprehensively.

I was trying to explain what happened to me, yet I failed.

I remember going to my oldest sister and asking, "What does it mean when a man is on top of you?"

She asked, "On top of you doing what?"

I replied, "He said, now I'm gone give you the real thang, come on baby girl."

She immediately jumped up and said, "Ma, Killa been raped!"

Still confused, I didn't know what rape was. As I grew older, I found out its definition. I blamed myself for not trying to fight back and for lying there and crying. I said stop, of course, because it hurt, but I felt worthless.

Thoughts of the incident marinated in my head at school all of the time. I couldn't sleep at night, and I went without treatment for my entire childhood. My rape and molestation followed me into adulthood and affected my mental and physical health.

After being raped, I was molested by my stepfather for the first time. It happened while in the bed with my mother. The only difference between this incident and the other one was that he didn't just hurt me; he also hurt my oldest sister.

After molestation, I went through two abusive relationships — one as a teen and the other as an adult. As a teen, we fought, and he slept around. I was living a grown-up life while in high school, and although I maintained my grades very well, I should have been more focused on my education. We were in and out of court all the time. I had a child by him, and things only got worse. He was jealous hearted, he gambled, and he was immature.

After this relationship, I started dating an older man. I thought he would know how to treat my children and me, but he ended up being the worst thing that could have ever happened to me. The hurt and pain that he inflicted was far worse than any rape, molestation, or physical contact. The first time he physically put his hands on me was when we moved to Texas. He choked me because I had received a twenty-dollar wire transfer from my son's father, money that I needed to purchase pampers. He would take my money. We were living on the streets for some time, and everyone I reached out to for help turned a blind eye.

There was this outreach center in Texas that assisted the homeless. I went there for help, but they turned me around. One worker ripped the application up in my face and assumed that I was lying because I didn't look homeless. She wasn't aware that I only had what I carried in my purse. I would go to a local grocery store and allow my children to eat fruit as we walked the store to keep cool. She didn't see my children and I asleep in the family restroom of that grocery store. She never saw me bathing my children or washing their clothes in the public bathroom and drying them with the hand dryer.

As I got my children and walked out, she followed us out. She yelled my name, "Ms. Wilson!" In relief and thinking that she was about to help, I turned around. She ripped up the application and threw it at me, saying, "Here's your trash!"

My life got worse before it got any better. Abused women hide their hurt, and become frustrated, incapable of thinking realistically, and unable to make rational decisions. My sexual abuse did not end as a child. My life was a broken puzzle with missing pieces until I noticed I needed mental support and referred myself to a clinic. Sexual assault can have many short- and long-term effects on mental health. As an adult, I still have flashbacks of my attack, and feelings of shame, isolation, shock, confusion, and guilt. I learned that my childhood was hindering me in life. It kept me from love, and when I did find it, I pulled away.

Now, I serve others by sharing when I find it appropriate. Through sharing, I encountered people that went through far worse. I can let go and let God handle it. I consider my life circumstances a blessing. I am stronger yet still fragile. At night I often think of the relationships I had with men. The majority of them were horrible. I made up my mind that I wanted better and started teaching men how to treat me. I won't settle for anything because I realize that I am a queen, and in the end, I am the token.

Dear Young Woman,

You don't have to become a statistic. If you've experienced abuse of any kind, I urge you to listen to my testimony and know that there is light at the end of each dark tunnel. I thank God daily for restoring the missing pieces to my puzzled life, which is His Grace and Mercy.

Shequite Johnson, born and raised in the Mississippi Delta, the most impoverished region in the poorest state. She is both an overcomer and an abuse survivor. She has faced many challenges throughout her life with courage and determination. She has used her story to inspire others, especially young people, to believe in themselves and use every experience - positive or negative -- for motivational energy for forward movement.

Throughout her career, she has worked in various helping professions where her role was pivotal to community betterment and individual self-actualization. She is a wife and mother of three children, who are the joy of her life, and mentor and role model to many.

She balances a full-time job as a Human Resources Assistant for the Sunflower Consolidated School District. She is also a full-time student in pursuit of a Doctorate in Public Policy at Jackson State University, where she is an honor student. She makes her home in peaceful surroundings along the outer fringes of Indianola, Mississippi.

Cycles Are Meant to Be Broken

"How did I get here?" is a question that stopped me in my tracks. I was searching for answers as to why I couldn't resist the trap that the enemy had placed continuously before me. Once again, I'd landed myself in another situation that deep down inside I wanted to stay away from, but it seemed as if I was continuing in yet another cycle.

I could identify my thirst for attention and my longing for male companionship. But the thing about it is, my broken heart had yet to heal, and I wasn't disciplining myself enough to renew my mind. So, there I was again, in another "situationship" where I'd given pieces of me to someone who didn't care.

That longing for attention came from the rejection I experienced as a little girl. Hearing the words, "She isn't mine" as a child affected me in ways I failed to realize. Those words made me feel as if I wasn't

loved or accepted. In my mind, I had to fight for the attention I wanted, so that's what I did. And guess where it landed me: losing my virginity at sixteen and becoming entangled in a cycle dictated by lust.

Why was I always being rejected? One thing I didn't realize is how the enemy had established a plan for my life. I was blinded to the fact that the root of rejection was holding me captive. I continued to believe that something had to be wrong with me and that no one loved me—not even those close to me. And guess what? The enemy kept adding fuel to the fire.

There were some childhood memories that I blotted out only to relieve me of the trauma they caused. Here's the thing though, if not confronted, the very things we try to hide or choose to forget about will make a grand appearance again, and we can either face them or continue to ignore them. Our decision will lead to our healing and deliverance or continued bondage.

Fast forward quite a few years, I remember one morning that I was excited to read about the woman at the well—you know, the one who had five husbands. As I positioned myself on the floor in front of my Bible and notebook, I was ready to dig in. As I started reading John chapter four, tears began to stream down my face. At that moment, memories that I chose to forget came rushing in like a tidal wave. The words "Just lay there" echoed in my mind as I remembered my small body pinned underneath a boy older than myself at the time. Even though I knew what he was doing wasn't right, I felt as if I didn't have a voice, so I just laid there. After he was done, I thought what he did was acceptable, even though there wasn't any penetration. That opened the door to more than I wanted, and it was apparent as I got older.

The other memories made me realize that I could have very well been that woman that Jesus was talking to because I'd been in a dysfunctional cycle as well, going from man to man. I guess we both needed an encounter with Jesus so that we could know that He sees us and He's aware of everything that has taken place in our lives. Better yet, He came so that we wouldn't have to live in such a way. We just needed to know we had His attention.

You can say that deep down inside all I wanted was love and acceptance. I just needed someone to rescue the little girl that was slowly dying inside—the one who screamed for attention but didn't get it. I thought that if I gave myself to a man, that proved his love for me. But that wasn't true. It led to heartbreak, guilt, condemnation, and the worst of all—soul ties. Not only that, I would still feel unfulfilled and emptier than before the ordeal. All I could think about was why this again? What was wrong with me? Why was this cycle continuing in my life? Had I not had enough? Was I not paying attention to the signs? What was wrong with me?

So many questions and it would take some searching to get to the bottom of things. You see, I've always been attracted to men in some way and longed for their attention. It's like there was something I had to prove about myself. I guess you could say it became my coping mechanism. There was something great that I desired but deep down inside, it wouldn't come from a man! It would only come from God.

I continued the cycle until one day; I got fed up with myself. I got tired of the empty confessions. I got tired of the guilt and shame. I got tired of lying to myself and God for that matter. I was fed up, and I wanted to see a change, and I knew what I had to do. I didn't want to die in my sin, so I made up my mind to cut ties with my past and begin again. I had to renew my mind daily and remind myself that God put me here for a purpose, and it wasn't to be caught up in dysfunctional cycles.

Dear young woman,

Cycles are meant to be broken. Jesus came that you may have life and have it more abundantly. You may see the trend in your life or maybe even notice some that have been passed down generationally. It can stop with you. They can end with you. You know why? God is a cycle-breaker, and if you yield to Him, He can make all things new in your life.

I want you to be mindful that you are precious even when others can't see it and when you can't fully perceive it. Your worth is not contingent on the things of this world but on the sacrifice that Jesus made for you. You are loved, and the love that God has for you is unconditional and everlasting. You are enough, so don't allow anyone's opinions of you cause you to feel worthless. You don't have to continue in cycles. You can live a life totally surrendered unto God. But here's the thing, you have to decide to do so. What will your decision be?

 **Shameka Nicole** was born and raised in a small town in Mississippi. Growing up, she developed a passion for writing not knowing how God would use her gift to impact many people. Many of her early writings expressed her cries for help as she was suffocating under the weight of rejection.

Years later, her works are still effecting change in the lives of others. As a writer, it is her prayer that her works will point others to the heart of God in hopes that they will experience His love and care for them.

Shameka sees life as precious and her motto is "How you view your life will determine how you live it." She wants others to see the value of life by encouraging them to make the most of it and by living out their God-ordained purpose.

Blog—www.preciouslife1.com
Facebook—Shameka Nicole
(www.facebook.com/shameka.nicole.332)
Instagram—@redeemed_restored; @precious_life1
Twitter—@PreciousLife_1
Email—nicole.shameka@gmail.com

Thank God for Growth

The famous quote, "If I knew then what I know now," definitely applies to my life. You see I made a lot of bad choices early on, choices I feel could've been prevented. But you know what they say, "If you know better, you do better." I guess I didn't know any better.

Growing up, a single mother raised me. Don't get me wrong; she did the best she could. Most of my life, she worked two jobs to support us. Because my mom worked so much, it gave me a lot of time to do what I wanted. Looking back, I can only wish that my mom had more time to focus on us and push us to our full potential. But being a single mother, I know her time and resources were minimal. I love my mom, and she did the best she could. Because she was raised very poorly, she did better than the odds that were against her. My mom didn't have the best example of a mother in her life to show her how to be a mother, but she turned her life around and started living for

God. This blessing transferred over to me and made me the woman that I am today.

Although I made a lot of bad choices, my mom, being a godly woman and raising me to have a relationship with God, helped me to turn my life around. However, it took years of bumping my head and making several wrong choices to realize that I needed to do this. All of my problems started when I began looking for love in all the wrong places. I was longing to have the love that I didn't receive from my father, I loved my father dearly. I enjoyed being around him and I wanted to be with him more than I could. But the facts are that he let it be known early on in my life that he did not want me. My mom always told me, my dad, wanted her to have an abortion because they were in college and having me would ruin their life.

Well, my mom decided to have me, and he decided to leave her because of that decision; and they were never together again. I knew my dad loved me, but when I was around him there was always this feeling of rejection. I always felt like he didn't accept me. Those feelings caused me to be very promiscuous early on. By the age of thirteen, I had lost my virginity to a guy that was much older than me. I always dealt with men that were older than me and allowed them to take care of me. I think this had something to do with wanting my dad to love and take care of me. I started running away and being very disobedient to my mother.

By the age of fifteen, there was not much my mother could do with me and I ended up pregnant with my first child. Having a child slowed me down for a little while, but by age sixteen, I left my daughter with my mom, and I began reverting to my old ways. By this time, I was very much out of control and living a very dangerous and unbecoming lifestyle. I ran from man to man and was in toxic relationships involving sex, drugs, and alcohol.

I have three children with two different men, and both of those relationships were toxic. Because I didn't know my worth and I was still longing for the love that I never had, I accepted a lot of things that I should not have. All of my relationships have been dysfunctional and very toxic. I have children with two of those toxic men and til this day our relationships are still very dysfunctional. I can't even hold a decent conversation with them, let alone co-parent with them effectively.

Although I love my children, I wish I had made better choices as it relates to their fathers. Some advice that I wish someone would've given me that I can share with you is to please be cautious of the men that you have children with. After all, we have to deal with these men for at least eighteen years out of our child's life. Plus, our children can also inherit some of their father's dysfunctional ways if we're not careful and prayerful over them. To save yourself some headache, if you don't currently have any kids, wait until God blesses you with the husband that you know is worthy of fathering your children. I would not want anyone to be in the positions that I found myself in. No matter what hand we are dealt in this life, we have to choose to create better experiences. A lot of women have the same issues- generational

curses, daddy issues, rejection issues, self-esteem issues, emotional issues, and the list goes on.

We have to be in control of our destiny and not let our issues or dysfunctional upbringing keep us stagnant. We are daughters of royalty and our father is the king of kings, so we must rise up and be the queens that God has called us to be by any means necessary. If you are a younger queen, develop a relationship with God and get a mentor that can help guide you the right way. If you are an older queen like myself, please know that it's never too late to start over. God will meet you right where you are and help you the rest of the way.

Dear Young Woman,

Know your worth because I know mine now. I am a single mother of three who has recently obtained my bachelor's degree. I am patiently staying celibate and waiting on God to bless me with my king. I leave you with this scripture, Matthew 6:33, "Seek ye first the kingdom of God and everything else will be added to you."

 **Ebonee Monique Bursey** was born and raised in Memphis, Tennessee. She spent most of her childhood growing up in a small country town of Henning, Tennessee. She currently resides in Dallas, Texas.

She is a single mother of 3 children Destiny, Carnelius and Carmelo whom she adores. She recently obtained her bachelor's degree in Organizational Leadership in August of 2019.

Ebonee is a lover and follower of Jesus Christ, who is working on discovering her passion and the calling of God on her life. She stands on the scripture Jeremiah 29:11, knowing that God has a great purpose and wonderful plans for her life.

You can follow her on Facebook at Ebonee Bursey send her an email at eboneebursey@gmail.com

Empty Place

*J*ust send it. I can't do it. Just do it. I can't. What will people say?

How do I explain when I don't fully understand it either?

DO IT AND GET IT OVER WITH!

As I have this pep talk with myself, it's still unreal to me that this is happening. Now it's done. Where do I go from here? The most important question is, how did I get here? Last week I had plans to marry the man of my dreams and here I am now informing everyone that the wedding is off and that he, my husband to be, called it off. I can feel those old feelings of rejection resurfacing. I can feel that dark place beckoning and calling my name ever so faintly. I can feel the tug, the pull, and the all consuming emptiness of that place long forgotten.

The empty place, the place that robbed me of my sense of security, of my self-worth and my identity. It was in the empty place that I forgot who I was. It is also in this place where my psyche was most damaged. In this place is where I began to believe that how others treated me was a reflection of who I was. It was also here that I started a journey of self-destruction, one that I barely escaped with my life and my mind intact.

Like a roadmap of time, I can trace my abandonment issues back to my childhood. I don't know if it was a specific incident or a culmination of several things that caused me to be affected by the spirit of rejection. At exactly what point did my hopes, dreams, and belief in myself die? I wasn't certain, but die it did, and in its place was an insecure and unsure girl. Those feelings of unworthiness would taint and ultimately infect every area of my life.

I found myself in relationships that weren't the best for me. I've worked jobs that didn't require me to push myself and passed up careers because I didn't think I had what it took to succeed. I even compromised in some places because I didn't think I deserved more- more respect, more love, or more out of life.

As women we automatically internalize rejection and pain. We somehow feel as if we lack in some way when a relationship doesn't go as planned, as if it's our sole responsibility to make things work.

As I began to cry out to God and ask Him, "Why did this happen to me?", I can remember Him so vividly responding, "You're asking the wrong question. The question is not, why did this happen to you, but rather why did this happen for you?!" I was floored!

It amazed me that I had been holding on so tightly to the very thing God was trying to pull me apart from! Something instantly shifted in my spirit, and my understanding was enlightened! I felt the peace that surpasses all understanding that the Bible speaks of. I cried tears of joy and gratitude at the mere thought that God loved me so much that He was willing to break me so that He could build me into the woman that He created me to be! My God!

Like Pharaoh and the children of Israel, God had hardened my fiance's heart towards me. He knew that would be the only way I would be released from what He had not ordained. God knows us so intimately and deeply, the real us, the part of us that we don't allow others to see, the parts of us that we can barely stand to face.

My fear of rejection and abandonment threatened to send me back to that empty place, but God. My insecurities from past failures and mistakes allowed me to settle for things that were beneath me. I thought I had too much baggage to ever have the life I so desperately longed for and dreamed about. Who could love a woman as damaged as me? Past mistakes and failures rendered me incapable of hoping for a life I so desperately craved for. The constant reminder of terrible choices always seemed before me.

From societies standpoint, I was considered a failure, a disappointment. I was a high school drop-out and had given birth to four chil-

dren out of wedlock before the age of twenty-one. I had battled addiction, was a convicted felon that had served prison time and suffered the death of a child that I was never able to truly deal with. It seemed as if I had too much behind me to ever move forward. The very weight of it threatened to suffocate and kill the hope that was within me. I had to make a conscious decision, and a determined effort to seek God concerning my burden, a burden that had become too much to bear.

As I began to seek God's Word about who I was, I became more confident in His love for me. I realized that there wasn't anything I could do to earn His love and that His love just was. I also had to forgive those who had hurt me and acknowledge my wrongdoing. To doubt myself was likened to doubting God. It implied that God was wrong about me. I know that God does not lie and that what He said concerning me was true, that His plan and purpose for my life would not change. It didn't matter if I wasn't currently feeling that way, and what I had been through in my life hadn't changed that. Other's opinions of me didn't change it; and my mistakes, failures, and shortcomings didn't matter.

There is absolutely nothing in life that you can go through and not come out of. Not only can you come out, but you can thrive and become a beacon of light for other wounded souls. I've embarked on a journey of discovery. Not a journey of self-discovery, but a journey of discovering who I am in God and confronting those toxic traits within myself. I was in search of the day that I could look in the mirror and not be haunted by my past mistakes and failures. I've decided to move through life lighter. I'm no longer straining under the extra weight that I had been carrying around; and I'm no longer haunted by guilt, shame, disappointment, and unforgiveness.

Dear Young Woman,

The task of discovering one's true identity can seem insurmountable and overwhelming; and sometimes it'll seem easier to settle where you are. I dare you to tap into your purpose and find YOU!

Tyra Cyprian is a mother and grandmother who resides in Hammond, LA. She is the founder of " Against All Odds" a non-profit organization that is geared towards disadvantaged and disenfranchised youth.

Through various struggles and hardships, she has made it her mission to help those who deal with their silent pain. She strives to be a beacon of light to those trapped in the darkness of pain and despair. Tyra's prayer is that through authenticity and transparency, women everywhere will find the courage to live out LOUD!

23

Never Looking Back

A beautiful home and a beautiful family is all that I ever wanted, but that all came to a screeching halt when I heard, "Get out, I don't need you!" Those were the words I heard while loading my car with clothes, my children's toys, and other necessities that I could get my hands on.

Lord knows I didn't want to leave, but I had no choice. It was time for me to go. The tears were rolling down my face as I hurried back and forth to pack our things. My children were too young to understand what was going on, but eventually, I had to explain why we were leaving our home, or at least what I thought was our home.

If I could only wake up from this nightmare, it would all be over. If only I didn't have to hear my husband say those words to me. Yes, my husband. How could the man I dated for over ten years treat me this way? How could the man that asked me to be his wife say such horrible words to me? Why did I stay so long to endure the disrespect, lies, and abuse? Why? Unfortunately, I didn't have the answers.

This was not easy for me. I experienced so many emotional breakdowns. I went from feeling like a failure to feeling unloved. I even begged and pleaded with him to let me come back so that we could be a family and take steps to work on our marriage. See, this wasn't the first time. Sadly, in the past, I had left multiple times, but I always went back. Of course, he said all the right things to lure me back in because he knew he held the key to my heart. I even enrolled us in counseling and reached out to his pastor for help. Needless to say, things only became better temporarily.

The ride to my mother's house was silent. So many thoughts were racing through my head. I was an emotional wreck. I tried so hard to hold back the tears, but it was impossible. Why me God? What did I do wrong? I prayed and prayed for God to restore my marriage. I prayed for this man to love me. I did all that I could do. That day I felt like God wasn't on my side, and I did not understand why all of this was happening to me. What did I do to deserve this?

My mother was waiting for the kids and me as we entered the door. She greeted the children with a hug and smile. I was too afraid to look her in the eyes because I felt ashamed. The last thing I wanted to hear was, "I told you so." Instead, she said to me, "Daughter, I love you." I can still hear her speak these words today. I burst into tears as she hugged me tightly. All the love I needed was right there. I thank God every day for my supportive family and friends.

I knew my mother was at peace because her grandchildren were no longer living in an unhealthy environment. It was time to put my feelings and selfishness to the side and put the best interest of my children first. I no longer wanted them to hear the yelling and screaming from their rooms. My children shouldn't have to see their mother cry herself to sleep, or not able to explain where my husband (my son's father) was because he left for days at a time. My children were not being raised in a loving and caring home, and there was no way I could let them suffer any longer. I was so caught up wanting my husband to love me, that I was blinded by what I was doing to my children.

I needed God to work on me, but most importantly, I needed to work on myself! I couldn't accept living this way any longer. Yes, I was removed from the situation, but I still lacked inner peace. Then one day, I realized that being taken for granted wasn't love, and neither was manipulation or abuse. As the months went by, I had to make the decision to save me! It was time for a change.

I came to terms that this marriage was over, but that didn't mean that my life needed to be. I was determined to take my life back. My entire perspective about my life changed. I no longer viewed myself as a failure because I had to move back in with my family, but instead, I looked in the mirror and saw a woman of courage, and a woman who gained strength from her trials.

My experience from this marriage put me on the path to finding myself. I was lost, and only God was able to allow me to be found. It was a difficult journey that I needed to take. During this journey, beautiful discoveries were made. I discovered my self-worth, happiness, and peace. I learned that it's okay to be a single woman, and it's okay to raise my children alone because God is my strength, and through Him, I can do all things. I was able to provide my children with a nurturing and caring environment.

Knowing that they were happy is what fueled me to become better and focus on moving forward. It was such an amazing feeling to rise from that dead situation! My children no longer suffer from what I thought was love. Overall, I was transformed into a new woman, mother, daughter, sister, and friend. Thank you, Lord, for making me brand new and giving me the strength to never look back.

Dear Young Woman,

If you are currently experiencing a feeling of hopelessness or can't seem to find your way out of a toxic situation, I encourage you to seek God in prayer and listen for His voice. If He says move, then you must do so. It may not feel right, and your heart may be tied to a situation, but God knows what's best for you.

You may not recognize it at that moment, but it will all make sense in due time. Believe me. You may feel as if you're taking steps back, but God is setting you up to move forward. You must take the initiative to recognize that it's time to go further. Once I realized this, I never looked back. I will never forget the pain I endured, but now I'm completely done with letting it dictate my future and define who I am.

**Renata Rafiel** is an educator, blogger, and founder of Purposeful and Pretty, a platform created when God gave her this vision to encourage and uplift women through inspirational writing. Her platform is a community designed to connect with women who are searching for their God-given purpose.

As a single mother of two children, she yearned to discover her purpose. After many years of searching in all the wrong places, she never gave up on her dream. Becoming a blogger wasn't on her list, but as she used God's gift, she learned that writing was her true calling.

Besides managing her platform, she is the author of an e-book titled "Purpose Points." Renata is also working on a variety of writing projects that are scheduled to release later this year. Be sure to stay connected with Renata on her journey of faith and purpose.

To learn more about Purposeful and Pretty, please contact Renata

www.purposefulandpretty.com
purposefulandpretty@gmail.com
@purposeful_and_pretty

Do I Still Have Value After HIV

Growing up in my community, it was customary to seeing violence. It could be economical, gender-related, or social coupled with poverty; there was nothing more that I wanted than the freedom to escape to all these "nightmares." As though it was not enough, I witnessed how traditionally, women were left to be passive in decision making, and being vocal or speaking up would be regarded disrespectful. These experiences created fear in me that if I don't do anything to change that narrative, I will become a victim. I hoped my escape would come from working hard in school, so I could get a chance to be well, become better, and help address such issues.

What I did not realize was, I had more significant problems to deal with, such as self-esteem, self-awareness, and being confident in my individuality as a young woman. I did not realize that due to the environment I was growing up in, my self-esteem had already been ruined and to worsen it, at the age of sixteen while in my twelfth-grade year, I learned that I was HIV positive. I can still that fateful day learning about my status and how it made me feel life had come to an end.

Dealing with living positively with HIV didn't seem like a possibility as it is today. I was heartbroken and felt worthless. All I wanted was to die. I remember having thoughts of throwing myself on the road to be hit by a car would be much easier than to live. What was more heartbreaking was the fact that during those days, it was more common to think that a girl who is HIV positive is promiscuous. This was so shameful to bare even though it was not my case. How I got infected still feels like a mystery.

After those moments of sobbing and hoping for relief of some sort, I thought I had come to terms with it, until boys would ask me out, only to reject me after discovering I was HIV positive. The first time it happened I thought that maybe I didn't know how to break the news, or maybe it was just one of those things where I had met someone who didn't understand what it meant to be HIV positive. Life went by, and it happened, again and again, the rejection. At that moment, a bell went off for me. Maybe something was not well with me, and I couldn't bear it.

As a teenager, my self-esteem was ruined, and I felt like I didn't deserve anything good or better. I began to feel like an outcast. I slowly started withdrawing from crowds and didn't want to be noticed by anyone of the opposite sex. I was afraid of being rejected again. Inspite of this, there was a man who persistently chased after me. I didn't like this man that much, and I tried to use my status to scare him away, but he still accepted me.

I wasn't so sure if this was even what I wanted or if I was looking for affirmation and dealing with peer pressure, so I decided I would talk to him, but I wouldn't stay in the relationship for long. I kept the promise I made to myself. I was suffocating, so I managed to get out, but my quest for affirmation and validation was still alive and later led me into a relationship with a man I had only met on social media. Everything seemed so sweet and real. For a young woman in her early twenties, I was in love and thought this was it until I learned that he was married with a child. I would describe this relationship as chasing the footprints of a ghost. Who can see the footprints of a ghost?

You see young woman, the chase to be validated, is often coupled with vain emptiness, which if not dealt with before you find your purpose or take a journey to self-discovery, can lead to your being vulnerable, mistreated, and devalued. It can also cause you to compromise your values. No matter how much we may want to go against God's ideal way of dating, we should learn to listen to that still small voice who is always speaking to our heart.

These experiences caused me to question, "What do I want in a relationship? Is it companionship?" I learned that I needed to know myself first. I continued to ask myself, "What makes me excited? What motivates me?" We draw ideal happiness and wholeness from things that excite and motivate us.

When you know what makes you happy, you won't wait for someone else to make you happy. Before anyone approaches you about dating or courtship, you should know yourself and know that you are an automatic follower of what gives you life, and that is God, the divine. He is the filler of all voids.

Dear Young Woman,

You must appreciate yourself first. When you understand who you are and what you are, you are more likely to get into a healthy relationship. Thus, it is vital to have a healthy mindset. How good you are to yourself is evident in a relationship by the choices and decisions you make. No matter what we go through, we should never think that the challenges take away our value.

What we go through does not define us or take anything away from us. Your situation does not matter, you are still beautiful and deserve the best. In my case, being HIV positive made me feel like I did not deserve anything good. I felt equal to scrap metal. I was not looking for a man who would see my value. I wanted my finding a man to add value to who I was.

You must know that personal freedom, happiness, validation, and affirmation, is in your power. It is a journey every young woman should take to discover her true identity and God's ideal plan for her life. I didn't know how to be me because I didn't accept myself for who I was. It's important to accept where you are first and find your purpose. When you find your purpose, you will be whole, and it will give you will power to champion your emotions so that you will never feel like a relationship is what will make your life full or complete.

Winnie Mabena is a civil registrar, an international speaker, and author. She is a magazine contributor at onetribemagazine.com, a mentor and coach. She specializes in empowering others to live above life's challenges and develop a positive mindset so they can live their lives positively.

Winnie is usually referred to as "The Living Positively Brand" and "Living Positively with HIV" full of positivity. She is the Founder and executive of Living Positively Brand, an organization that empowers others in mindset shifts and decisions making. Her organization also coaches, mentors, advises, and writes mostly for personal development.

She holds a double major Bachelor of Arts degree in Library and Information Science and Public Administration and a Diploma in Management Studies from the University of Zambia. She has a certificate in Self Discovery and Personal Development and currently pursuing her professional course in teaching methodology.

Visit Winnie Mabena at her virtual home here
https//:www.livingpositivelybrand.com

Rejection Veil

2 Corinthians 3:16- 18 NIV, "But whenever anyone turns to the Lord, the veil is taken away. Now the Lord is the spirit, and where the spirit of the Lord is, there is freedom. And we all, who with unveiled faces reflect the Lord's glory, are being transformed into his image with ever-increasing glory, which comes from the Lord, who is the Spirit".

A veil is a garment worn to cover the head and face of an individual. It blocks others from seeing what's beneath. I was once veiled, tricked into thinking I was not good enough, I wasn't worth anything, and anybody who walked into my life would surely walk away. The veil I wore was rejection.

Before my preteen years, I was raised in a two-parent home. Both my parents worked and provided for my sister and me. My father had issues that would haunt me for years to come. He was an alcoholic and drug abuser, but I didn't really understand this until I was older. He would come home smelling like an alcohol distillery and verbally abuse my sister and me. The devil was beginning to unravel and cut the relationships between the Heavenly Father and my earthly relationships.

You see words can cut like a sword and stay embedded in your brain for a long time. My father would tell us that we wouldn't amount to anything or that we were a pile of human waste. You see, he was speaking things into existence without knowing the power of the tongue. Even though he abused us verbally, we still loved him. He was our father, but it wasn't enough love to make him stay in our lives. As I look back, I'm glad it happened the way it did because this situation could have turned out worse. God removed the mess and turned it into a message.

My father walked away when I was eleven years old. I was hurt and very upset. I couldn't understand why my daddy had to leave us. He cut the relationship bond between a father and his daughter. This was the beginning of my "daddy issues," rejection issues, and several attempts by the devil to keep me veiled. A year after my parents' divorce, I started being very disobedient. I would hang out with the wrong crowd, stay out late, and do the complete opposite of what my mother told me to do. I was brilliant in school, but I cut class just to hang out. In my mind, I knew everything, so I decided to run away.

My mother had no clue about the whereabouts of her child. I was not even a teen yet, but I was going to another city with a friend. His father picked us up and off to the city we went. Now that I reflect, his father never asked about my parent's permission or anything of that nature. Once we got to the city, my "friend" left me alone with his father to run errands.

Well, this grown man that was my father's age decided he was going to rape me. He took full advantage of my situation. I was stuck in a city with no family and just one friend. I was underage and knew nothing about being on my own. To keep me quiet, he gave me some hush money and eventually sent me back home on a Greyhound bus.

I felt so much shame because this happened to me. The physical and emotional pain led me to blame my father. If he had been a present and nurturing parent, this would never have happened. Where was my fatherly protection? I never told anyone about this situation.

After the rape, I started feeling like I had a hole missing within me, like pieces of a puzzle that couldn't quite fit into their prospective place. I couldn't understand why I felt so empty and alone. During my childhood, I didn't go to church unless my great-grandma Gee took us. Church was never a significant factor growing up, so I never really knew about Jesus until I was eighteen years old. The spirit of rejection was slowly beginning to take hold of me. In addition to my feeling weird within physically, my body began to change into that of a grown woman, even though I was only eleven years old. My face may have looked young, but my body screamed something entirely different.

The newfound attention from this new body made me feel awkward at first. Eventually, I figured out that all this attention was what I thought I was missing because I no longer had my father's interest or attention anymore. Grown men way older than me would stare and try and talk to me. I was no longer a rejected little girl; now, I was beginning to feel a false power behind my looks. I noticed how guys would go out of their way for me; and how I didn't have to walk home from school by myself anymore.

The things I desired from my father were presenting themselves through the actions of men and boys. This false sense of contentment was really forming the garment that would hang over me for many years to come.

It took years to overcome my fear of rejection. I smiled through my pain as a coping mechanism. God kept allowing things to happen until I faced my fear. Even when I didn't think anyone cared, and I was dealing with life alone, God was there orchestrating my victory. My father in heaven showed me unconditional love. He reminds me daily that I'm a daughter of a King, and there is nothing I have done wrong that will change His love for His child.

Dear Young Woman,

Never allow your past to blind who you are. You may have felt rejected, but God will turn the rejection to projection. Those life experiences that tried to destroy you will project you into your destiny and help someone else along the way. You are not alone. Remove the veil and be free!

**Tashina Brown** is a first-time author and speaker in the making. Tashina desires to help women unveil their true potential. Before writing, Tashina worked 13 years in the Finance/Banking industry in many roles. After having a successful career helping many people improve their financial areas of their lives.

Tashina now aspires to support women who have gone through the birthmother/ adoption process and strives to create ways to allow them to heal. Tashina enjoys traveling, music, and desserts. Tashina is available for bookings and speaking engagements. You can reach Tashina at 804-647-8027 or email her at info@godlyclout.com

Nothing Happened

My sisters and I were at our neighbors' house getting our hair done. I was asked to go into the room across the hall to grab some hair products. When I entered the room, he came in behind me and shut the door. He tackled me and wrestled me to the floor. He held his hand over my mouth as he attempted to undress me. I quickly became emotional as I imagined what was going to happen next. I started crying and pleading for him to stop. Seeing how hysterical I had become, he ceased and began to apologize. I was so frantic that I ran out of the house.

In the following weeks, I tried to avoid him, which was very hard because he frequently visited my boy cousin. I decided not to speak of the incident because, after all, nothing had really happened. I still felt very uncomfortable around him. He would always stare and smile when he saw me. Again, I never spoke a word. He, however, decided to dispel his love for me to my boy cousin. As if it wasn't hard enough having to be around the guy, my cousins began to tease me about how in love B was with me. Eventually, I allowed my fear to dissipate. Somehow, I reasoned that it was just a misunderstood boyhood crush. After all, nothing had really happened.

Summer 2005, we spent many days home alone, just my two sisters, older cousins, and me. My older sister and boy cousin had a habit of playing tricks on my little sister and me. Perhaps, this time the trick went a little too far. My grandparents were gone for the day, and despite being told that we could not have company, the boy next door came over to play video games. My sisters and I were sitting on the couch, watching television when he walked into the house. Obviously still uncomfortable, I retreated to my bedroom.

"Denise, come here!" my boy cousin yelled. I reluctantly walked back into the living room and stood back from my cousin's bedroom door. "B just wanted to say hey," he said. I turned around to walk off. "Hey, come back here. Why you can't speak?" I reluctantly said hi. After a few hours, I ventured back into the living room and started playing with my siblings and cousins.

"Denise, B wants to talk to you. I think you guys should go into the room and talk." "No, thank you," I said as I began to head back towards my room. As I attempted to retreat, my cousin grabbed me and began to drag me into his room. I fought him, playfully, but I had let my guard down. As the door locked with both of us on the inside, my mind began to wander. "He'd let me go last time." "He knows I'm not interested in him." "He isn't going to hurt me," I thought. He tried to kiss me, and I fell onto the bed while attempting to push him away.

My body froze as the scene unfolded. I didn't scream. I didn't say stop. I just lay there as tears rolled down my eyes. He pinned me down with one hand and undressed me with the other. He began to whisper in my ear about how I had been teasing him for months. I recall thinking when he couldn't actually get it in, that I could grab the lamp from the dresser and hit him across the head; but instead, I didn't move, and he raped me. When he was done, I simply lay there until he fixed himself and left the room. Then, I went into my room and cried myself to sleep.

When I woke up, my grandmother was home. I replayed the events in my head as reality sank in. I was hurt, embarrassed, afraid, and completely in shock. The hours after I told her what had happened were a blur. She called the police, and fear began to consume me. "What now?" I thought. The officer questioned us about the events that had taken place. He replied, "Are you sure you want to go through with this?" I reluctantly said, "Yes." I don't know how I knew, but I felt like they didn't believe I was being truthful. As the officer went next door to take a statement from B, my grandmother began to question me. I'm not sure that I actually heard the words that were coming out of her mouth, but the invalidation set in. To further negate my statement, the officer returned in pure disbelief. "Ma'am, are you sure that the boy next door did this?" "He's a little fella," the officer said. I felt my heart drop to my stomach. Not only was I raped, but neither my grandmother nor the investigating officer believed me.

It took me over ten years to accept:

1. Something did happen.
2. It was not my fault.

For years, I walked around silent, angry, fearful, and misunderstood. In high school, I was *easy* because I never wanted to experience that entire process ever again.

Your story may not be my story, but we all have a story to tell. Emotions, thoughts, and fears are all secondary to being. We exist, thus we must learn to co-exist with what and how we feel and think. Many of us live in bondage to the inability to discuss things that have happened to us. Yet we continually feel, think, and respond based on our experiences.

Dear Young Woman,

You may have been silenced, but your freedom is found in your words. Please realize that no matter how long you have been in bondage, it does not mean that you have to stay there. We can define what we go through by calling it purpose, or we can continually allow it to define us by taking on the labels of our circumstances. I refused to be labeled as a victim of sexual abuse.

However, I continuously re-victimized myself by choosing to *willingly* have sex when I, in fact, did not want to. I was a child when the initial incident took place, but as I matured, I began to understand that I no longer had to accept that *nothing happened*. No, I am not a survivor because I did not simply survive the abuse. I thrived despite…

Be you. Be heard. Be free. Approval is not needed.

Denise Nicole is a 26-year-old mother of three from South Louisiana. She currently holds a Bachelors Degree in Social Work and is pursuing a Masters in Counseling.

She was taught that education is the key to success. After many life lessons, she realized that education does not merely pertain to what is learned through institutions. She now seeks to share this philosophy with the world.

She possesses experiences far beyond her years; nonetheless, through faith and resilience, she has overcome and is still overcoming. Her greatest ambition is that by sharing her journey, others too can thrive despite their circumstances.

Denise Nicole is a self-proclaimed writer, blogger, and advocate for change, mental wellness, and self-betterment. Feel free to follow her on social media or contact her via email. Rest assured that she is simply human, just like you.

Blog site is: https://approvalisnotneeded.weebly.com
Instagram: _ApprovalisNotNeeded

Words from Alandria...

It's my prayer that you are uplifted after reading the stories written by these amazing women. It took a lot for these ladies to muster up the strength to remove their masks and uncover secrets that they worked hard to bury and tuck away. It is also my prayer that you realize that we as women all have something in common. This book was written to inspire you and hopefully encourage you to remove your mask and boldly share a piece of your truth with another woman.

The Bible reminds us that we overcome by the blood of the lamb and the power of testimony. My question is, what power can an unspoken testimony provide? Your past has power. Your story may be the key to unlocking someone from an emotional prison. You endured the test, but your testimony is for someone else. I dare you to share your story of how you were able to triumph after the trial.

As a certified Personal Development Life Coach for women, it's my job to push women into their purpose. Your story has a purpose, so I'm pushing you to tell it. However, if you are having trouble over-

coming or moving past certain issues in your life. I'd like to invite you to work with me. I have an 8-week coaching program, *"Mask Off: A Journey to Freedom…"*.

In this program, you will learn how to:

- Overcome the things that have tried to overtake you
- Remove your mask
- Profit from your pain
- Walk in freedom and much more…

For more information, please visit bit.ly/MaskOff2019

Made in the USA
Middletown, DE
13 February 2020